person-to-Person
building a relationship with God through prayer

Also by Mack Stokes

The Bible and Modern Doubt

The Bible in the Wesleyan Heritage

The Epic of Revelation

The Holy Spirit in the Wesleyan Heritage

Major United Methodist Beliefs

Questions and Answers about Life and Faith

Scriptural Holiness for the United Methodist Christian

Theology for Preaching

person-to-Person
Building a Relationship
with God through Prayer

Mack B. Stokes

PLOWPOINT

Breaking Ground for the Seed of the Gospel

person-to-Person: Building a relationship with God through prayer
By Mack B. Stokes

Copyright © 2007 by Mack B. Stokes
All rights reserved.
ISBN-13: 978-0-9762277-4-8

Published by Plowpoint Press of Graham, North Carolina.

For permissions, information or to order more copies please contact:
Plowpoint Press
PO Box 979
Graham, NC 27253
336.226.0282
866.269.2421
www.plowpoint.org

Publisher's Cataloging-in-Publication
(Provided by Quality Books, Inc.)
Stokes, Mack B.
Person-to-person : building a relationship with God
through prayer / Mack B. Stokes.
p. cm.
ISBN-13: 978-0-9762277-4-8
ISBN-10: 0-9762277-4-6

1. Prayer--Christianity.   I. Title.

BV210.3.S76 2007   248.3'2   QBI07-600183

Library of Congress Control Number: 2007931394

Dedication
To Susannah Rose Stokes,
named for her grandmother,
Rose Yow Stokes.
For the encouragement and love
she gives her grandfather.

Contents

Foreword

Some of us may remember the days when our long distance communication options were often defined by placing a person-to-person call. Today, we live in a society and time where our ability to communicate is more vast and varied than ever before: telephones, cell phones, fax machines, voice mail, email, snail mail, text messages, teleconferences, web conferences–and the options expand almost daily. However, both statistics and experience tell us that our relationships are only more challenged and threatened than any other time in history.

More than ever, our marriages are struggling, our families are dissolving, and even our churches are splitting and closing. In our work with churches and pastors across denominational and geographical lines, we encounter similar problems over and over again all stemming from broken and hurting relationships. Sociologists and psychologists remind us that communication is essential to a healthy and functional relationship. But why hasn't our advanced technology improved our ability to truly communicate? Could it be that we have forgotten the root of what real communication is?

The word "communication" stems from the Latin root *communis* from which "community" and even "communion" also derive. Therefore, inherent in communication is the essence of community and communion evoking intimate fellowship with another. So, communication cannot be defined by the technology which is used. Instead, true communication is all about the relationship. Without relationship, there is no meaningful communication, and without communication, there is no meaningful relationship.

Prayer has often been described as communication with God; however this communication cannot be merely defined by techniques. Instead, Bishop Mack Stokes aptly describes prayer as:

> **an interpersonal communion with God. Our finite souls are communing with and encountering God in person-to-Person experiences.**

In the following pages, Bishop Stokes presents a faithful and persistent study of prayer as Divine-human encounter through which our relationship with God and others is developed, nourished, and strengthened. *person-to-Person* goes beyond any limitations of a "how-to" book. Instead, these words invite us to venture deep into Scripture and into the heart of God to find a place of abiding–a place of intimacy–that is offered to us in the I-Thou relationship in prayer that can be applied practically in our daily lives.

The eternal principle of a person-to-Person connection is defined by our finite relationship with our Infinite God. Prayer is the bridge which allows this person-to-Person connection. As teacher, spiritual leader, and faithful servant of our Lord, Bishop Stokes employs the wisdom and insight given to him to help build this bridge of relationship by faith. Our families need this bridge. Our churches need this bridge. And our world needs this bridge.

May God richly bless you as you build your relationship with God through prayer.

Rev. Beth M. Crissman
Shepherd of the Vision, The Ministry of Plowpoint

Words of Affirmation

I have always prayed. However, this book has revealed to me how to connect with God in a new way, a very personal way. My person-to-Person connection has strengthened my faith and hope for the future.

Susannah Rose Stokes
United States Naval Academy, Class of 2011

As I read this book I feel as if I was once again in a class taught by Professor Mack Stokes. Professor Stokes is the one who taught me about the nature of God and the nature of humankind. Through the years the challenging lectures, assignments and sermons of Reverend, Professor, Doctor and Bishop Stokes have been a lifeline for me.

Now, through reading and studying *person-to-Person,* the call to go deeper comes again. This work leads one to understand our utter dependence on God and at the same time opens a deep awareness of God's personal love and call to a great destiny. This relationship comes through prayer, the heart of religion. It is here that the intellect and the soul are connected with God.

There is a great hunger in America for meaning, purpose, joy and love. Each chapter in this book is a spotlight in the stadium of life. The answer to our deepest needs and yearnings are exposed to the light of Christ so that it is possible to see how "God's Kingdom can come on earth as it is in Heaven."

I recommend *person-to-Person* as a way to experience life now and future. In this "ongoing pilgrimage we can receive from God the power to see life through with joy and hope."

Evelyn Laycock, Doctor of Ministry
Professor Emeritus, Hiwassee College
Founding Director, Lay Ministry Center,
Southeastern Jurisdiction of the United Methodist Church

When I became a United Methodist bishop, someone said to me, "Friend, you are about to discover new dimensions of prayer." That prediction has proved true. To lead the Christian life, to lead the church, one must lead through prayer.

We could have no better guide and teacher than Bishop Mack Stokes. Professor Stokes taught generations of Emory University students how to think about and how to follow Jesus. He is someone who lives the life of prayer, a pastor who values the scriptural word above all others, and someone who can lead us into new dimensions of prayer. In this tightly packed, wonderfully biblical meditation on prayer, Bishop Stokes gives us the proof of a lifetime of seeking and listening to God.

William H. Willimon
Bishop of the United Methodist Church
Birmingham Area

In this book on prayer, Mack Stokes provides a comprehensive theological and pastoral approach to a subject that receives too little solid theological treatment. Too often the subject of prayer is treated in a superficial manner as an optional devotional practice. This book, however, reflects on prayer as integral to the human experience of the Transcendent and Personal God. This book takes objections to prayer seriously and responds to those objections with reason and sensitivity.

The great strength of this reflection on prayer is that it grows out of the author's life-long experience of praying and his exceptional intellectual gifts as a theologian. Mack Stokes life and witness are living examples of the meaning of prayer!

Kenneth L. Carder
Bishop of the United Methodist Church
Ruth W. and A. Morris Williams Professor of the Practice of
Christian Ministry, Duke Divinity School

———————————————

person-to-Person is a wonderfully comprehensive yet accessible discussion of prayer for all those who seek to deepen their understanding of the Christian faith. This book tackles the tough, tender, simple and perplexing questions many of us ponder over but frequently don't ask out loud. Individuals and groups alike will benefit enormously from this engaging book.

Jan Love
Dean and Professor of Christianity and World Politics
Candler School of Theology
Emory University

———————————————

Bishop Mack B. Stokes has taught us for decades about the importance and power of prayer. In this book, Bishop Stokes provides an expansive exploration of the subject that is sure to teach and inspire all who seek deeper communion with God through prayer. Prayer, that wonderful place where 'the intellect and the soul are connected with God' is explained in a wonderfully accessible manner to all who pick up this book.

Lovett H. Weems, Jr.
Distinguished Professor of Church Leadership
Wesley Theological Seminary, Washington, D.C.

Thomas Merton observed that most of us live with blaring televisions, squawking radios, clanging computers and a myriad of distracting noises–and we like it. Quiet frightens us, Merton said, because it is in the stillness that we hear God's voice inside us, and we are overwhelmed by its power. Mack B. Stokes takes us back to the source of power and reintroduces us to the possibility of a person-to-Person relationship with God, and to the opportunity of listening for God's response. Conversing with the Creator of the universe may be scary at first, but the relationship changes our lives forever.

Rev. Bob Edgar
General Secretary
National Council of Churches USA

Bishop Stokes is first and foremost a teacher and an apologist for the Christian faith. He is at his best in this book as he centers his mind and heart on prayer. Anyone who is committed to a growing relationship with God will profit from this book. Anyone who is struggling with the discipline of prayer will find immeasurable help.

Maxie D. Dunham
Chancellor
Asbury Theological Seminary

From the Author

It has been my privilege to work with Plowpoint Press and Beth and Kelly Crissman. I am grateful to Beth Crissman for the depth of her understanding both of my thoughts and the hearts of the readers. This is seen in the quality of her "Questions for Reflection" at the end of each chapter. I am thankful to God also for her having a well-informed, communicative mind and heart into United Methodism.

I am grateful also to Kelly Crissman for his mastery of detail and practical good sense in bringing together this book for publication. I stand before him amazed at the spiritual and intellectual depth in grasping what vital experienced religion is all about.

To you, the reader, I pray for God's blessing of wonderful grace to be with you as you explore the richness of a life of prayer. Thank you for reading this book and your willingness to study and share in prayer. The greatest compliment you could pay me is to begin praying and to continure praying. Pray for your church and your pastor and do not stop until you stand in the presence of God.

Mack B. Stokes
Bishop of the United Methodist Church
Lake Junaluska, North Carolina

One

Prayer as the Heart of Religion

Religion concerns the relationship between God and us. Raising questions such as: What does God have to do with us? What is God's purpose for us? What do we have to do with God? How can we open our souls to God and receive God's blessings? How can we work together with God? How are we related to others through God? What does God have in mind for us after death? These are religious questions.

Why are these questions distinctively religious? The answer is because these questions are asked in no other areas of human life. For example, in business such questions are not asked unless the people involved happen to be religious. They are not the questions labor asks. We do not ask them when we are developing skills to do a job and make a living. Public schools, colleges, and universities do not exist to ask them. Museums of art, libraries, and sports arenas have their roles, but they do not raise religious questions. Romance, too, though one of the important human interests is not by itself religious.

So religion is a unique sphere of life. And prayer is the heart of religion where the intellect and the soul are connected with God. For in prayer we stop talking about religion and enter into a relationship with God. Therefore, prayer, in its highest form, is communion with God.

Creature Seeking the Creator

When we pray, we can be opened to and sense the presence of

God. We feel ourselves drawn to the One who made us. We feel our utter dependence on God and stand in awe of God. At the same time, we have the mysterious awareness of this God's personal love. We know that the God who made us loves us. We know that the God who knows us cares for us.

In prayer, we know that God calls us to the new life. God not only knows and loves us: God summons us to a great destiny. And, in our ongoing pilgrimage through this present life, we receive from God the power to see life through with joy and hope. In prayer, then, we feel this strangely profound experience of awe and dread mingled with adoration and love. We know that without God we would be nothing. We are aware of our nature as a creature, and in that awareness we lift up our hearts to our Maker and Redeemer.

Religion, then, far from being just another experience, is another kind of experience that has a power to shape all others. Through prayer all other areas of life may be influenced and enriched. In moments of prayer–sometimes gradually and sometimes suddenly–we become aware of the ineptness of any of the offerings of this world to satisfy our deepest needs. For only God can probe the depths of our being and meet those needs which cry out for an answer.

Without religion, this connection with our Creator is left out. And without this connection we cannot be fully human. We are like creatures living yet only partly living. Our life lacks any enduring foundation. Without this connection, we feel like passing whiffs of insignificance. The great fourth century African Christian writer Augustine knew this when he wrote what is perhaps the greatest sentence ever uttered outside the Bible:

**You have made us for you, O God,
and our souls are restless till they rest in you.**

By virtue of our nature as human beings, we are endowed with a capacity for responding to God. This capacity, like other capacities, comes to expression as life goes on. It is nurtured or stifled, as the case may be, by environmental factors. But it is no more created by them than is the capacity for arithmetic, music, art, or athletics. The desire and need to respond to God presses forward through all kinds of environmental circumstances. Throughout the history of religion, various phrases have been used to identify this human quality. Some have called it our religious nature. Others have referred to it as our religious intuition, or our religious consciousness.

**God alone abides
as other things come and go.**

Hungering for the Abiding

There is much evidence supporting the idea that human beings have a kind of intuitive awareness of God. We perceive that the finite points to the Infinite, the passing calls for the Enduring, and the imperfect cries out for the Perfect. We are always observing things that come into being and pass away. Flowers wither away and die. Our dogs and cats, though precious, grow old and die. Friends come and go. We ourselves join all those creatures great and small which come into existence on this earth and then pass away. It is even more so with all our material attachments. Cars run down and have to be traded away. When we die, our fondness for carefully selected pieces of furniture, or houses, or farms, vanishes like passing gusts of wind. These grim certainties are perpetual reminders of our finite nature. In our human situation we perceive, by a kind of direct insight, that *GOD IS*. We don't have to prove that God is, we simply proclaim it. God alone abides amid the things that come and go. Often this experience emerges as a kind of dim consciousness of the Infinite. And sometimes it bursts forth into an inspired prayer of absolute faith in God.

This is what Henry Lyte the Scottish hymn writer must have felt when he prayed:

> **Swift to its close ebbs out life's little day;**
> **Earth's joys grow dim, its glories pass away;**
> **Change and decay in all around I see;**
> **O thou who changest not, abide with me.**

In prayer, this mysterious, intuitive certainty comes home to us. For as we pray we feel ourselves to be in a direct and life-giving relationship with the One who is from everlasting to everlasting. It is here, then, that this mysterious unique sphere of the religious comes alive for us and in us. For God is known, loved, adored, felt, and responded to when we open our souls to the divine Presence. God communes with us and we with God. In prayer, God meets us where we are and summons us to the new life. And there we begin to see that everything we are and do receives enduring meaning and glory from the God who made us for the divine purpose.

Breaking Open the Fullness of Prayer

Understanding how we encounter God and God encounters us can open up the fullness of prayer. All true prayer is person-to-Person communion with God. It involves trustful dependence, gratitude, adoration, confession, petition, openness to God, decision, and love. It includes the sustained desire to understand and do God's will in spite of counteracting impulses. During certain moments of prayer, the word "communion" is inadequate when God encounters us and we encounter God. Such times are when, like the psalmists and Jeremiah, we pour out our souls, our fears, our despair, our struggles, and, as a result, we are moved into a more vital relationship with God.

In prayer, there is also an awareness of how God is affected by us–God's displeasure with us, God's enjoyment of us. For God is hurt by our wrong attitudes and failures, and God is blessed as we are blessed. This mysterious fellowship with God, like all true friendships, is an end in itself. And, it is more than that. Nevertheless, it stands in its own right and is self-authenticating.

Prayer as Petition

Often we first encounter God in prayer by asking God for things. Petition is a basic element of prayer, but it is only one such element. There are many levels of our petitions. They may be crude and petty or refined and magnanimous, and the quality of our prayer-life can be measured in part by the quality of our petitions. When reduced to mere selfish entreaty, prayer may become a source of doubt. Why? For two reasons. First, as life goes on, we learn that God does not always grant our requests. If a mother prays for her son to recover from a serious illness, and he dies, her faith may be shaken. Second, doubts arise when we think primarily of prayer as petition because we lose sight of the deeper meaning of prayer, namely, communion and encounter with God.

It is still true, however, as Jesus taught that entreaty has its worthy place in prayer.

> *Ask, and it will be given you; search, and you will find; knock, and the door will be opened for you.*
>
> **Matthew 7:7 NRSV**

Deeply rooted in our Christian heritage is the conviction that we are to make our requests known to God.

> *Don't worry about anything; instead, pray about everything. Tell God what you need, and thank him for all he has done.*
>
> **Philippians 4:6 NLT**

Our Lord's Prayer contains petitions relative to both our physical needs and our moral and spiritual needs. Therefore, no understanding of prayer can be adequate which does not include petition in it.

Prayer as Ritual

Some people think of prayer as ritual. They think chiefly of the words used, the forms followed, the routines practiced. Prayer means "saying prayers," reading prayers, or counting prayers. In its cruder forms this understanding of prayer borders on magic. For it is often supposed that we can affect God by going through certain routines. For many devout people who pray, ritual may lead them into authentic experiences of communion and encounter with God. Nevertheless, there is always the danger of stressing formal exactness more than the living person-to-Person relationship with God.

Prayer as a Quest for Truth

Still others have given us wide varieties of definitions of prayer. In each of these there is real groping for a deeper understanding. Some say that prayer is a quest for truth. Prayer is understanding. Others say that prayer is "the soul's sincere desire, uttered or unexpressed." Immanuel Kant, the eighteenth century German philosopher, spoke of it as a "heartfelt wish." Again, there is the view that prayer is emotion. It is feeling a certain way toward God and the universe. For a large number of people, prayer is contemplation or meditation. And for others it is simply aspiration or the longing and reaching for the ideal.

Each of these ways of looking at prayer has some truth in it, but each fails to grasp the essential reality of prayer, namely, communion and encounter with God. Prayer involves ritual but only as a means to communion and to the life-giving relationship with God. Prayer implies the quest for understanding, but understanding by itself misses the unique dimension of the experienced presence of God. Prayer, on one side, is desire. But we have all sorts of desires. Desire is not connected with prayer until it aims toward God and is fulfilled in God. Contemplation, meditation, and aspiration are all factors in creative prayer. But, by themselves, they are merely human processes. They become living forces in prayer when we feel we are in the presence of God.

Formal exactness of ritual can not replace the person-to-Person connection with God.

Prayer as Belonging to God

Many people today fix their attention on the merely human.
Their vision of God, if it exists at all, tends to be blurred
or obscured by their ceaseless study of themselves, their
problems, and their surroundings. Therefore, they miss the
mysterious depths of Christian experience. The quality of our
experiences is largely determined by the quality of the realities
we encounter. When we see an ant hill, we feel one thing.
When we stand before the Rocky Mountains, we feel another.
Vast oceans roll between those whose experiences are confined
to the merely human and those who feel that they are in the
presence of God.

From prayer in the biblical heritage, we receive many
blessings. One of the most precious of these is the sense of
belonging to God. We know our true identity. We are no
longer mere products of nature. Nor are we just members
of a family or community. We are not simply psychological
creatures with all sorts of tendencies, impressions, and
impulses. Rather, in prayer we are given the marvelous
awareness that we are the children of God. Everyone knows
the painful experience of being left out. We know what
it is not to belong. And yet, in prayer we experience the
overwhelming sense of belonging to our heavenly Father.

The blessings of the life of prayer are not merely momentary:
they come from growth in the practice of prayer. All authentic
men and women of prayer made it a lifelong process. For
them it meant pressing forward in understanding God's holy
purpose for them and in responding to the divine summons.
In this total process, they became increasingly aware of God's
delight in this divine-human relationship.

Prayer as Response to God's Will

The inevitable fruit of this person-to-Person communion and encounter with God is a resounding yes to God's call to let God do a wonder work through us. And, of course, this means service to our fellow human beings. Prayer is communion and encounter with God in which the soul turns toward God and responds to God's will. Since character and conduct emerge from our profound inner experiences and relationships, it follows that creative service will flow from the life of prayer. For God is not only to be adored and enjoyed; God is to be obeyed. God has overwhelmingly important goals which are to be realized through us. In the life of prayer and service, Jesus Christ is our Source and Model. Through prayer the Holy Spirit acts within us to fill us with the love of Christ. And in this way we are given by grace what John Wesley, the eighteenth century English preacher, theologian, and founder of the Methodist movement, called that "inward holiness" which leads to "outward holiness."

Understanding Why We Pray

There are three primary reasons why we should pray. The first is that God commands it and wants us to do it. The second is that our human needs require it. The third is that God advances the Kingdom by it. Now, let us consider these.

God Wants Us to Pray

God wants us to pray, so God calls us to it. Our Creator knows our hungers and needs. God knows the purpose for which we were created and placed on this earth. God made us to enter into a life-giving relationship with our Maker by faith, and this relationship involves prayer. In the Old

Testament, God's call to prayer comes primarily through the example of the great leaders of Israel. All of them—from Abraham to Moses to Deborah to Hannah to Samuel to David to Elijah to Job and to all the prophets—all were people of prayer. In particular, the psalmists expressed the heights and depths of this Divine-human relationship through their grand words of prayer.

When we come to the New Testament, we find that Jesus and the apostles called us to pray both by their example and precept. Jesus led the way by his own life of prayer. He was praying at the time of his baptism:

> *One day when the crowds were being baptized, Jesus himself was baptized. As he was praying, the heavens opened....*
>
> **Luke 3:21**

He prayed during the forty days when he went into the wilderness and was tempted by the devil:

> *When Jesus returned from the Jordan River, the power of the Holy Spirit was with him, and the Spirit led him into the desert. For forty days Jesus was tested by the devil, and during that time he went without eating.*
>
> **Luke 4:1-2**

Often he withdrew from the crowds to pray:

> *But Jesus would often go to some place where he could be alone and pray.*
>
> **Luke 5:16**

> *When Jesus was alone praying, his disciples came to him...*
>
> **Luke 9:18**

> *About eight days later Jesus took Peter, John, and James with him and went up on a mountain to pray.*
>
> **Luke 9:28**

> *When Jesus had finished praying, one of his disciples said to*

26

him, "Lord, teach us to pray...

Luke 11:1

He prayed all night before choosing his disciples:

About that time Jesus went off to a mountain to pray, and he spent the whole night there. The next morning he called his disciples together and chose twelve of them to be his apostles.

Luke 6:12-13

He prayed for Peter that he might not be destroyed by Satan:

But Simon, I have prayed that your faith will be strong.

Luke 22:32.

He prayed for his followers–including those in succeeding generations:

I am not praying just for these followers. I am also praying for everyone else who will have faith because of what my followers will say about me.

John 17:20

He prayed at Gethsemane:

Jesus walked on a little way before he knelt down and prayed, "Father, if you will, please don't make me suffer by having me drink from this cup. But do what you want, and not what I want."

Luke 22:41-42

He prayed on the cross:

Jesus said, "Father, forgive these people! They don't know what they're doing.

Luke 23:34

Jesus also called his followers to pray. Knowing the awesome power of temptation, he said:

Stay awake and pray that you won't be tested. You want to do what is right, but you are weak.

Mark 14:38

He called upon his disciples to pray for God to send laborers into the harvest:

27

> *So pray to the Lord who is in charge of the harvest; ask him to send more workers into his fields.*
>
> **Matthew 9:38**

These were his instructions to them:

> *The harvest is great, but the workers are few. So pray to the Lord who is in charge of the harvest; ask him to send more workers into his fields.*
>
> **Luke 10:2**

One of the Master's important summons was to pray for one's enemies

> *But I say, love your enemies! Pray for those who persecute you!*
>
> **Matthew 5:44**

In addition, Jesus urged his followers to pray the special prayer which he taught them.

> *Pray like this: Our Father in heaven, may your name be honored. May your Kingdom come soon.*
>
> **Matthew 6:9**

Following in the footsteps of Jesus, the apostles also became leaders in the call to prayer. And Paul summarized this in when he said:

> *Pray without ceasing.*
>
> **First Thessalonians 5:17**

In a true sense, the whole Bible has been for Christians the Word of God calling them to the life of prayer. One of the most important reasons for reading the Bible devotionally is that it helps us to know that we are in the presence of God, for God speaks to us in the Holy Bible. And through the Bible, God provides that spiritual atmosphere in which we can enter into the living communion and encounters with God.

How easily we forget that we were made for God and that

without God we grope in the dark! God has revealed the divine unalterable reasons for calling us to pray and even for persuading us to do so. The Holy Spirit wants us to know God is there. In every era people have been distracted because there are, in our human nature, natural impulses that pull us away from God. In these times of continuous distractions, the most compelling reason for praying is that it pleases God for us to do so. For it brings countless blessings to us and abounding joy to the Great Heart of God through the person-to-Person relationship.

The world's attractions lure us away from God. Prayer draws us to God.

Before taking this thought further, several clarifying comments are needed. For one thing, we need to keep clearly in mind who calls us to pray and why. God is not a tyrannical cosmic ruler ordering us about as though we were slaves. We are rightly repulsed by the idea of a divine tyrant who demands that we lose our selfhood and self-identity. The Holy One who summons us to pray is our Creator who called us into being and invites us into relationship. This is an invitation to be in relationship with God, our Creator. God made us, knows us, loves us, strives with us, and delights in our existence and in our full humanity. So our Maker, who loves us most and knows us best, calls us as free beings to respond readily to the divine love in prayer. As soon as we hear this as God's way of seeking us and longing for our best, our whole attitude changes.

God makes no threats or legalistic demands of us. Rather, God's call is person-to-Person. It is not merely an order addressed to society. As the Bible teaches, it is an intimately personal word addressed to each one of us. God summons you and me to pray. Through Jesus Christ, this comes to us as God's personal invitation. It is an expression of God's interest and love. Our part, then, is to respond by praying and growing in the practice of prayer.

Furthermore, God's command to pray is not made once and for all. It is not to be understood as something carved in stone, fixed and rigid. On the contrary, the command to pray is living, personal, ever new and fresh. For God always takes into account the vital human interests of each new day and every new situation.

Another thought bears directly on God's summons to pray. This is the idea that even God is enriched by our prayers. God delights in our responsiveness and rejoices in our cooperation. God enjoys communion and encounter with us. In Psalm 141 the psalmist acknowledges that the prayers offered are *as incense offered to you.* Even though this may sound like some strange new teaching, it is an often overlooked biblical truth about God. Otherwise, why is there the talk in the Old Testament about God's wrath and disappointment with the people of Israel and with particular individuals? And why was Jesus weeping over Jerusalem or hanging on a cross? The only adequate answer must include the thought that God delights in our appropriate responses and, otherwise, is profoundly hurt and saddened by our wanderings from God's purpose and desire for connection with us.

We Require It

The second reason for praying is that our human nature and sense of loneliness require it. In fact, our sense of loneliness calls for it. People often find it hard to understand their deep moral and spiritual needs. We cover up those needs and blindly refuse to face them. As life moves on, these deeper needs surface and are felt. Sometimes during a crisis we feel the need for God, and crises are sure to come. The loss of work and business failures make us think about deeper values. In sickness we become aware of how feeble we are, and in death is the grim reminder that some things are beyond our control. The breakdown of character, affecting both ourselves and those who love us, opens our eyes to the need for God.

The stark truth is this: As wonderful as our life on earth may be, it is fraught with uncertainty, failure, pain, and tragedy. Even when everything seems to be going our way, we still know that nothing which this world has to offer–however attractive–can satisfy the deep mysterious longing for God. As John Wesley mentioned in several of his sermons,

> **Amidst our plenty,**
> **something still, to me, to thee,**
> **to him is wanting!**

People can have great wealth, extensive properties, a good marriage, children, and the added gratifications from art, literature, culture, athletic events, and still we feel a sense of emptiness until we lift up our hearts in prayer and know that we belong to God.

Under many of the circumstances of life, our need for God

is so overwhelming that we cannot help praying. William James, the well-known Harvard psychologist and philosopher, summarized the situation in his *Principles of Psychology*.

We hear in these days of scientific enlightenment, a great deal of discussion about the efficacy of prayer; and many reasons are given us why we should not pray; whilst others are given us why we should. But in all this very little is said of the reason why we do pray, which is simply that we cannot help praying.

The basic point is that no one can struggle most productively through life's baffling circumstances without God's help. And none can rise to the highest levels of full humanity without divine assistance. If we are strong, we still need God's immeasurably greater resources to make us stronger. If we are weak, our weakness is made strong by God's grace.

But he said to me, "My grace is sufficient for you, for my power is made perfect in weakness." Therefore I will boast all the more gladly about my weaknesses, so that Christ's power may rest on me.

Second Corinthians 12:9 NLT

If we are cruel, hostile, anxious, and confused, our inner life can be transformed by the creative dynamics of the love of Christ. If we become weary in the tasks of life, God summons us to pray so that we may receive new resources for creative living.

The Kingdom Emerges from It

The third reason for praying is implied in the first two. God commands it and our human needs require it so that through prayer God's holy Kingdom can be realized in us and through us on earth. However, much more than prayer is needed to advance God's work in the world. It takes the fulfilled promise and presence of the Risen Christ in us. And it takes the power of the Holy Spirit manifest through Pentecost to empower and propel us to accomplish it. It takes the wisdom that the love of Christ implies. It takes people who have so opened their hearts to God in prayer that they are eager to identify God's will for them and to move where God is leading them. It requires a willingness to follow through with life-changing decisions. It requires Christian marriages and family life that are committed to pay the cost of obedience together. It requires healthy organizational structure. It requires Christian character in business, labor, the professions, the mass media, government, and in the total life in community. Our own best resources need to interact with God's grace for the highest glory of God and the blessing of human beings.

Prayer, therefore, is the vehicle through which all these other aspects are joined together for the purpose of realizing God's Kingdom here on earth. The Kingdom of God is the ultimate fulfillment of our relationship with the Creator where our person-to-Person communion is made manifest in and through the lives of the created. Through prayer, God becomes real in us, through us and among us. It is the very heart of our relationship with God. It is the very heart of our religion.

Questions for Reflection

1. Religion can be generally defined as "belief in and worship of God or gods, and a specific system of belief, worship, often involving a code of ethics." In what ways does prayer define our belief in and worship of God that moves us beyond a mere code of ethics?

2. How have you encountered your life of prayer:
    *   as petition?
    *   as ritual?
    *   as relationship?

3. How and when have you experienced God's "Kingdom come" through the transforming power of prayer for you or others?

*person-to-Person Connection**

*At the end of each chapter, this section is offered to help you, as the reader, begin applying this new knowledge in your personal prayer life.

Begin to examine your own life of prayer in both your practice of it and your purpose for it. Consider ways in which your prayer life can be enriched to strengthen your real heart connection to God.

Two

The Bible as Guide to Prayer

The Bible is our prayer book. It is our primary source and norm in understanding prayer, and it is our guide also in the practice of prayer. No other sacred writings compare with the Bible in the emphasis on prayer as communion and encounter with God. By searching other writings, we may find scattered references which are comparable to the emphasis the biblical writers placed on prayer, but they are few and far between. Friedrich Heiler tells us:

> **In the exposition of prayer in personal religion it is almost exclusively Biblical and Christian personalities that have to be taken into account. Christianity, including the prophetic religion of the Old Testament, is "the peculiar home of personal prayer."**

> **To be sure, prayer is the essential utterance of all the religions of the world; it is not an exclusively Christian but a universally human phenomenon. But the personal life of prayer, free and living intercourse with God, has its native abode in Christianity as it has nowhere else in the entire history of religion.**

Heiler acknowledges exceptions to this in non-Christian religions and adds that the records of their prayers can be regarded only as parallels alongside the incomparably richer testimonies of those in the biblical heritage.

The basic reason for this foundational role of the Bible in relation to prayer is seen in the personalism of the Bible. Personalism is a thought or process that is related to a person and implies conscious relationship. The Bible is personalistic from beginning to end as evidenced by three realities. First and foremost, there is the biblical revelation of God as the Ultimate Personal Spirit. Second, there is the biblical revelation of human beings as finite personal spirits or souls. Third, there is the revelation of prayer as interpersonal-communion and encounter with God. Our finite souls are communing with and encountering God in person-to-Person experiences. The I-Thou relationship is at the heart of the biblical teaching on prayer.

To understand better the biblical meanings of prayer, we must also regard two other possible meanings. On the one hand, we can regard prayer as a purely subjective phenomenon in which prayer is reduced to human beings talking to themselves. According to this view, there may be some value in prayer as meditation, self-analysis, and quiet reflection. But there is no communion and encounter with God, no person-to-Person relationship. Consequently, if prayer denies the reality of the personal God, then prayer is reduced to an illusion. We fall into this kind of thinking by viewing prayer as a psychological projection. In this case, we project our thoughts and merely imagine the reality and presence of God resulting in prayer being regarded as wishful thinking.

There are varieties of ways in which prayer is regarded as a merely subjective encounter. In response to all such views, where prayer is concerned, everything depends on the reality of God as the Ultimate Personal Spirit. Therefore, prayer is not subjective at all. If God is a personal reality in our lives–as the Bible teaches and our best thinking confirms–then the biblical understanding of prayer rests on solid foundations. Additionally, how can we sweep away, on the basis of a psychological theory, what has been confirmed in the personal experiences of millions of people throughout the centuries?

On the other hand, we can also move away from the biblical teaching on prayer by thinking of God in impersonal terms. In regard to God, some have said that God is the Ultimate One. Others have thought of God as a Being-in-and-of-itself. Still others have urged that God is Cosmic Process. Each of these thoughts, and many others similar to them, has the merit of affirming the reality of some kind of Ultimate Being or Process called God. But none of them opens the way to the kind of person-to-Person encounter of which the Bible speaks.

On the basis of these views of God as impersonal Being or Process, there have been mystical types of prayer. For example, some have moved toward absorption into the divine Being. And others have ascended the ladder of prayer to behold the glory and beauty of God as abstract Goodness. The history of mystical types of prayer has its value and glory. But, however meaningful in the lives of Christians and others, it takes people away from the primary focus of the Bible on prayer as a way to develop the person-to-Person relationship and grow in personal communion and encounter with God.

Supporting the person-to-Person Encounter

For those who want to turn prayer into a strategy for using

God for their selfish ends, the Bible offers no support. For those who are interested in prayer as mystical absorption into the divine Being, the Bible will not be their guide. This means the Bible is not pantheistic. Similarly, for those who think of prayer as a ladder of ascent toward God, the Bible will be only one among various guides. And for those who are mainly focused on the by-products of prayer—mental health, emotional healing, positive thinking, peace of mind, and even love—without regarding the demands implied in the personal encounter with God, the Bible will call for rethinking.

But for those who think of prayer as a responsible person-to-Person relationship with God—encompassing the full ranges and depths of our souls—the Bible is the supreme source and guide. Therefore, the Christian leaders in the life of prayer have immersed themselves in the atmosphere and spirit of the Bible. This is especially evident in their devotional writings and practices, and it is evident also when we survey the prayer books of the various churches. Through these prayer books, which received their inspiration and direction from the Bible, prayer as person-to-Person communion and encounter with God has been kept alive from generation to generation in local churches throughout the world.

The Influence of Biblical Writers on Prayer

Against this background, let us consider six ways in which the biblical writers, with their intrinsic personalism, have influenced the prayer-life of Christians.

Prayer as Awareness of God's Presence

First, the biblical writers affirmed their awareness of being in the presence of the God who mysteriously called them into being. Through this awareness, the biblical writers knew that God made them for a purpose, so they were not only to adore God, they were also to obey God.

Prayer as Awareness of God's Holiness

Second, the biblical writers were keenly aware of being in the presence of the holy God. Because of this undeniable holiness, they also knew that this holy God required of them actions and attitudes that reflected God's holiness including love, justice, mercy, and peacemaking. As a result, this realization has had a profound effect upon Christians in their prayer-life across the centuries where the prayers of God's people called for action and reform that would reflect their holy God.

Prayer as Practice of Community

A third factor in the influence of the biblical writers upon succeeding generations of Christians was their practice of prayer in community. Their personal encounters with God were experienced communally. This is seen in the Old Testament in the covenantal ties binding people together under the God of Abraham, Isaac, and Jacob. In the New Testament this communal experience centered in the presence of the Holy Spirit who bound Christians together under their common Lord.

Prayer as Connection with the Christ and Our Eternal Security

A fourth influence on prayer from the biblical writers became real in the New Testament in the connection between prayer and Jesus Christ. Jesus himself established this when he taught his disciples to pray in his name. Jesus said,

I am the vine, and you are the branches. Those who remain in me, and I in them will produce much fruit.
If you stay joined to me and my words remain in you, you may ask any request you like and it will be granted!

John 15:5,7 NLT

If our prayers are defined by our relationship with Jesus Christ, then Jesus sets the standard for our prayers. Being joined to Jesus Christ and remaining in relationship with him binds our hearts and minds and souls to the will of God. Through this connection, two things happen. First, our prayers are aligned with the will of God, thus opening the vast opportunities of the Kingdom through our prayers. Also, by holding fast to Jesus in prayer, we experience the sense of Eternal Security. Through prayer, our relationship with Jesus Christ is greater strengthened and secured thus answering the great question: Where will you spend eternity?

Whoever believes in him shall not perish but have eternal life.

John 3:16 NLT

Prayer as Conduit of Service to Others

Through the assistance of the Holy Spirit, the apostles heard again and again the Risen Lord's call to give themselves in the service of others. This too has profoundly influenced the prayer-life of Christians by inspiring them to see the unbreakable connection between authentic prayer and service. Throughout Scripture, prayer has increased the awareness of God's presence, the awareness of God's holiness, shaped our Christian communities, connected us with Christ, empowered us by the Holy Spirit, and called us to service. These six elements in the influence of the biblical writers on succeeding generations of Christians are concretely seen in the prayer books, hymnals, song books, anthems, liturgies, and sermons of the churches which bear the name of Jesus Christ. The role of prayer in the Bible has shaped who we are and what we do as Christians throughout history. In the next four chapters, we will explore further writings of and about individuals in the Bible whose lives were shaped by prayer.

Prayer as Reality of the Holy Spirit

Fifth, the apostles and other early Christians influenced later Christians because they felt the presence of the Holy Spirit as a dynamic reality in prayer. Far from being impersonal, the Holy Spirit was known and experienced by them to be personal. The illuminating presence, guidance, and assistance of the Holy Spirit profoundly and mysteriously enriched the apostolic experience of prayer. Through the Holy Spirit the apostles and others held fast to Christ as central in their prayers. And through the assistance of the Holy Spirit, they heard again and again the Risen Lord's call to give themselves in the service of others. And this too has profoundly influenced the prayer-life of Christians by inspiring them to see the unbreakable connection between authentic prayer and service. The apostles saw, as none before them, that the purpose of the holy God for all human beings was to realize moral and spiritual values in community under the Lordship of Jesus Christ. Inward holiness produces outward holiness.

Questions for Reflection

1. How have you seen prayer be either:
   - purely meditative?
   - wishful thinking?

2. How does this negate an individual's personal relationship with God?

3. In what ways has your own prayer life become impersonal?

4. Think of a biblical story where an individual's prayer to God is undeniably a personal encounter.

person-to-Person Connection

Read the story of Nehemiah's prayer to God found in Nehemiah 1:1-11. Take note of what Nehemiah's prayer tells you about who God is, who Nehemiah is, and how his prayer is rooted and flows from his personal relationship with God.

Journal specific ways your own prayer life can be shaped by the prayers of Nehemiah.

Three

The Psalmists on Prayer

The Book of Psalms contains a wide variety of religious poetry that addresses the breadth and depth of our personal encounter with God. Some of the psalms are hymns of adoration and praise, and some are psalms of thanksgiving. A few contain communal lamentations; many more, individual lamentations. In addition, there are psalms pertaining to reigning kings, to Mount Zion as the holy dwelling of God, and psalms directed to ancient ceremonies and practices.

When we consider the variety of themes in the Book of Psalms, we see clearly that some of them do not give us guidance in understanding prayer. There are psalms that even plunge into the depths of vindictiveness. Nevertheless, it was with good reason that the earliest Christians joined the people of Israel in recognizing the glorious devotional heritage of the Psalter as the Psalms are also called. Christians learned from their experiences in the Temple and synagogues and used Israel's psalms in their own services of worship. Almost from the beginning of Christian gatherings in worship, congregations sang with words from the Psalms.

> *Be filled with the Spirit, as you sing psalms and hymns and spiritual songs among yourselves, singing and making melody to the Lord in your hearts.*
> **Ephesians 5:18b-19 NRSV**

Additionally, these ancient songs have shaped who we are and what we believe as Christians. As we look through a study

Bible or a concordance we can see how often the Psalms are referenced throughout the New Testament.

The psalms which bear directly on prayer as communion and encounter with God are those which express adoration, thanksgiving, lamentation, repentance, soul-searching, and trust in God's mercy and help. Let us now consider several important contributions of the writers of the psalms and their development of prayer in the biblical heritage.

Proclaiming the Glory of God

The writers of the psalms gave sublime utterance to the greatness and glory of God as the Ultimate Personal Spirit. We are told in Psalm 90:2 that even before Creation, God is *from everlasting to everlasting*. Psalm 104 lifts up the greatness and glory of God as the Creator who stretched *out the heavens like a tent, and. . . set the earth on its foundations.* God is the One who makes *the grass to grow for the cattle, and plants for people to use.* It is this God *who by understanding made the heavens* and *spread out the earth upon the waters.* (Psalm 136:5-6)

> *O Lord, what a variety of things you have made!*
> *In wisdom you have made them all.*
>
> **Psalm 104:24 NLT**

The psalmists were not focused on developing philosophical thought. Yet, by their inspired intuitions, they gave poetic voice to what philisopher Borden P. Bowne meant when he said:

In all our thinking, when critically scrutinized, we find self-conscious and active intelligence the presupposition not only of our knowledge but of the

world of objects as well.

This implies that wisdom is at both ends of the line. For though God is wisdom, God created all things, including our ability (or wisdom) to understand, if only in part, God and creation.

Proclaiming God's Steadfast Love

The psalmists also gave majestic beauty to the greatness and glory of God as the Holy One whose *steadfast love endures forever.* (The refrain from Psalm 136.) Here the goodness of the God of Israel comes into clear focus. And this absolute and steadfast goodness of God led specifically to the covenant with Abraham .

The primary purpose of many of the psalms is to provide functional guidance to shape the life of a faith community. One of the most conspicuous examples of this is found in Psalm 136. Where in response to the telling of God's mighty actions throughout history, the congregation repeatedly proclaims: *for his steadfast love endures forever.* The psalmists would not let Israel forget this marvelous love of God. Whether for their communal worship or their personal life, this statement of faith was affirmed and repeated throughout the Book of Psalms. It was a mighty, recurring theme in the poetic imagination of Israel that reminded the people who God was and the nature of God's enduring love. This repeated proclamation throughout the psalms has had a profound influence on the devotional and prayer life of Jews and Christians throughout the centuries.

For the king trusts in the Lord; through the unfailing love of the Most High he will not be shaken.

Psalm 21:7 NIV

The Lord leads with unfailing love and faithfulness all those who keep his covenant and obey his decrees.

Psalm 25:10 NLT

For your steadfast love is before my eyes, and I walk in faithfulness to you.

Psalm 26:3 NRSV

All kinds of troubles will strike the wicked, but your kindness shields those who trust you, Lord.

Psalm 32:10 CEV

Have mercy on me, O God, according to your unfailing love; according to your great compassion blot out my transgressions.

Psalm 51:1 NIV

Because your steadfast love is better than life, my lips will praise you.

Psalm 63:3 NRSV

For your love for me is very great. You have rescued me from the depths of death.

Psalm 86:13 NLT

Righteousness and justice are the foundation of your throne; love and faithfulness go before you.

Psalm 89:14 NIV

For the Lord is good; his steadfast love endures forever, and his faithfulness to all generations.

Psalm 100:5 NRSV

For as high as the heavens are above the earth, so great is his love for those who fear him.
But from everlasting to everlasting the Lord's love is with those who fear him, and his righteousness with their children's children.

Psalm103:11,17 NIV

Praise the Lord! Give thanks to the Lord, for he is good! His faithful love endures forever.

Psalm 106:1 NLT

Give thanks to the Lord, for he is good! His faithful love endures forever. Let them praise the Lord for his great love and for all his wonderful deeds to them.

Psalm 107:1, 31 NLT

For your steadfast love is higher than the heavens, and your faithfulness reaches to the clouds.

Psalm 108:4 NRSV

Be true to your name, Lord God!
Show your great kindness and rescue me.

Psalm 109:21 CEV

For great is his love toward us, and the faithfulness of the Lord endures forever.

Psalm 117:2 NIV

Let your steadfast love become my comfort according to your promise to your servant.

Psalm 119:76 NRSV

In your faithful love, O Lord, hear my cry; in your justice, save my life.

Psalm 119:149 NLT

See how I love your commandments, Lord. Give back my life because of your unfailing love.

Psalm 119:159 NLT

O Israel, hope in the Lord! For with the Lord there is steadfast love, and with him is great power to redeem.

Psalm 130:7 NRSV

I will bow down toward your holy temple and will praise your name for your love and your faithfulness, for you have exalted above all things your name and your word.

Psalm 138:2 NIV

> *The Lord is pleased only with those who worship him and trust his love.*
>
> **Psalm 147:11 CEV**

Proclaiming Adoration, Praise, and Thanksgiving

The psalmists' vision of God also shaped their call to prayers of adoration, praise, and thanksgiving. For it was that vision which led them to give to the whole world some of the most magnificent words of adoration ever uttered. And when, after more than two thousand years as Christians, we strive for words which express our sense of wonder and awe in the presence of God, we continually return to the words of the psalmists. They have taught us to adore God, to praise God, and to be filled with gratitude to God. No other words better express our true adoration, praise and gratitude to God than the Psalmists. Consider the following words which have been woven into our public and private prayers:

> *O Lord, our Lord, how majestic is your name in all the earth!*
>
> **Psalm 8:9 NIV**

> *Let the peoples praise thee, O God; let all the peoples praise thee!*
>
> **Psalm 67:5 KJV**

> *Every day I will bless you, and praise your name forever and ever. Great is the Lord, and greatly to be praised; his greatness is unsearchable.*
>
> **Psalm 145:2-3 NRSV**

Proclaiming the Approachability of God

At the same time, the psalmists have also taught us that God is altogether approachable. In the Psalms we know that God hears our prayers and that God is directly and graciously accessible.

> *I love the Lord, for he heard my voice; he heard my cry for mercy. Because he turned his ear to me, I will call on him as long as I live.*
>
> **Psalm 116:1-2 NIV**

Very little is found in the Book of Psalms about making blood sacrifices and offerings to God for our sins. Instead, we hear that God pardons those who humbly and truly confess their sins *for your name's sake* as found in Psalms 25:11 and 79:9. For *the sacrifice acceptable to God is a broken spirit* as we pray in Psalm 51:17 and also 32:5 and 40:6. The psalmists knew that congregations and holy places contribute significantly to the devotional life. But they also knew that God was already present within their own souls and ready to understand, to forgive, and to empower the repentant to respond. They sensed the presence of God and invited others to experience God's presence as well.

> *O taste and see that the Lord is good; happy are those who take refuge in him.*
>
> **Psalm 34:8 NRSV**

> *How sweet are your words to my taste, sweeter than honey to my mouth!*
>
> **Psalm 119:103 NIV**

Because the psalmists knew that God is directly accessible and approachable, they felt free to pour out their hearts to God. They reflected the many moods and struggles of people so fully that Augustine rightly called the Book of Psalms *an anatomy of the parts of the soul.* One evidence of this is that there are more than forty psalms of individual lamentations where the psalmist felt free to cry out to God from the pit of human despair. As examples, see any of the following Psalms 4-7; 42-43; 55; 64; 69; 88; 130; or 142. As the psalmists brought their deepest needs to God, mysteriously they found themselves experiencing the sustaining presence of God even in the midst of their struggles.

> *I will lie down in peace and sleep,*
> *for you alone, O LORD, will keep me safe.*
>
> **Psalm 4:8 NLT**

Some have said that the many psalms which use the personal pronouns *I, me, my,* actually imply a corporate or communal relationship with God. For, so it is said, the people of Israel thought of their communities as being individuals or corporate entities. However, to accept this view can also discount the personal relationship that is communicated. In those psalms, almost without exception, the person-to-Person relationship is self-evident. For example, the Twenty-third Psalm, though not a prayer, clearly expresses the thought that God is like a good shepherd to the inspired individual who wrote it. And the continuing glory of that psalm lies in the souls of the millions of people who feel the same caring love of God for them as solitary individuals.

Psalm 139 is one of the greatest prayers which reflects this person-to-Person relationship between God and a human being. The psalmist is keenly aware that God knows him through and through. God knew him before he was born and that God *knit me together in my mother's womb.* God is acquainted in intricate detail with all the ways of the psalmist. So, in the end, he cries to God, saying:

> **Search me, O God, and know my heart; test me and know**

my thoughts. See if there is any wicked way in me, and lead me in the way everlasting.

Psalm 139:23-24 NRSV

Even as readers we, too, can feel this. Augustine experienced it when he wrote: *What utterances I used to send up unto You in those Psalms, and how was I inflamed towards You by them.*

How our souls are moved to adoration and praise when we sing!

With all my heart I praise the Lord, and with all that I am I praise his holy name!

Psalm 103:1 CEV

This is the day the Lord has made. We will rejoice and be glad in it.

Psalm 118:24 NLT

The psalmists' many words of thanksgiving provided the inspiration for Martin Luther's insight: *The best way to lift the mind to God is to acknowledge and ponder past blessings.*

In times of deep despair what words can more perfectly express how we feel than these?

Out of the depths I cry to thee, O Lord!
Lord, hear my voice!
Let thy ears be attentive to the voice of my supplications

Psalm 130:1-2 KJV

The words of the Psalms give us words to use in our prayers. They give us powerful words, safe words, sublime words and even everyday words to use in our prayers to the God who wants us to be in person-to-Person connection.

Proclaiming a Model for Prayer

Again, one of the greatest contributions of the psalmists to prayer in the biblical heritage is seen in their inspired words, images, and model prayers. There is a mysterious power about their words and images. Where can we go to find more beautifully meaningful words in which to pray the sinner's prayer than these?

Have mercy on me, O God, according to your unfailing love; according to your great compassion blot out my transgressions.

Wash away all my iniquity and cleanse me from my sin.
Psalm 51:1-2 NIV

Who shall ascend the hill of the Lord? And who shall stand in his holy place? Those who have clean hands and pure hearts, who do not lift up their souls to what is false, and do not swear deceitfully.
Psalm 24:3-4 NRSV

And consider the following lines which have provided thoughts, words, and images for the prayer-life of millions:

So teach us to number our days that we may apply our hearts unto wisdom.
Psalm 90:12 KJV

I will pay my vows to the Lord in the presence of all his people.
Psalm 116:14 NRSV

The Lord is my light and my salvation; whom shall I fear?
Psalm 27:1 NIV

The Lord sets prisoners free.
Psalm 146:7 NIV

My times are in thy hand.
Psalm 31:15 KJV

Pray for the peace of Jerusalem!

Psalm 122:6 KJV

Lead me to the rock that is higher than I.

Psalm 61:2 NRSV

These and other words from the psalmists have been woven forever into the Christian vocabulary of prayer and devotion. They tell us of the soul's profound hunger and thirst for God. And they tell us also of the deep-seated need for God's supernatural help in the supreme quest of the spiritual life, namely, the love of God and of our fellow human beings.

Proclaiming Faith in the Triumph of Righteousness

The psalmists also teach faith in the ultimate triumph of righteousness. Without this, prayer would be reduced to a rope of sand which is gone with any wind of opposition. For if we are doomed to defeat at the start in seeking God and God's righteousness, where is the glory of the quest? The psalmists were confident that wickedness was like the *chaff which the wind drives away.* And they felt that *the wicked will not stand in the judgment* (1:4-5). God is holy and righteous altogether, and God alone is *from everlasting to everlasting* (90:2). Therefore, these ideas and models for behavior and commandments reflected in the Psalms are for all time

> *All he does is just and good, and all his commandments are trustworthy. They are forever true, to be obeyed faithfully and with integrity.*
>
> **Psalm 111:7-8 NLT**

The psalmists had good reason, the only decisive reason, for their confidence in their future. They based their hopes on

God's everlasting covenant of faithfulness.

Fret not yourself because of the wicked.

Psalm 37:1 KJV

My soul thirsts for God, for the living God.

Psalm 42:2 NRSV

Taste and see that the Lord is good!

Psalm 34:8 NIV

Be still and know that I am God.

Psalm 46:10 NIV

Suppose I had wings like the dawning day and flew across the ocean. Even then your powerful arm would guide and protect me.

Psalm 139:9-10 CEV

The quality of our character and prayer-life is seen in where we turn for help in moral and spiritual matters. What is the Source of our help? Is it work, or friends, or diversions, or a sense of humor, or gala events? One psalmist put it this way:

I lift up my eyes to the hills from where will my help come? My help comes from the Lord, who made heaven and earth. He will not let your foot be moved; he who keeps you will not slumber. He who keeps Israel will neither slumber nor sleep.

The Lord will keep your going out and your coming in from this time on and forevermore.

Psalm 121:1-4, 8 NIV

Amid all the things in life that come and go, the psalmists have taught us to put our trust in the one true God whose *steadfast love and faithfulness* are *from everlasting to everlasting.* As we look toward the prophets, the life of Jesus Christ, to Paul and the New Testament, we see that the psalmists, in addition to the glory of their enduring thoughts and words, prepared the way for what Jesus and the apostles taught on prayer. The time had not come for them to leave with us that fuller teaching on prayer made possible by the revelation of God as Father, Son, and Holy Spirit. Like the prophets, they prepared the way for the Savior.

Additionally, the psalmists offered us, as Christians, to use and to let their words flow into our prayers which we say in the name of Jesus Christ. They plowed up the soil of spiritual receptivity so Christians could receive the teaching of Jesus on praying for our enemies and for each other. And they helped Christians to be open to the illuminating and empowering presence of the Holy Spirit in prayer.

Questions for Reflection

1. The psalmists remembered and proclaimed the character and nature of God when they cried out in praise and prayer. How do our prayers reflect (or not reflect) the fullness of who God is?

2. The psalmists were also willing to admit their own frailness and failings in their prayers. How would our prayers be different if we truly acknowledged that God knew our innermost thoughts?

3. The psalmists also acknowledged that God was both the Sovereign Creator and an approcahable and accessible Advocate. How can our prayers reflect our relationship with our God who is both seated in heaven and present here among us?

person-to-Person Connection

Commit to read a psalm everyday and make this time of reading a personal prayer to God. Whenever the psalmist says *I* place your name. Or where the psalmist says *Your people* place the name of your church.

Four

Jeremiah on Prayer

Jeremiah has been called the first man of prayer known to the history of religion and the father of true prayer. People have been praying since the dawn of history. Why, then, do we have this special focus on Jeremiah? Primarily because Jeremiah was a great spiritual leader who entered into a creative, dynamic, sustained, person-to-Person prayer-life with God.

There were others who encountered such a prayer experience sporadically and yet others with some depth. Enoch walked with God. Abraham put his faith in God and entered into intercessory prayer. Moses was confronted by God and interceded for the people. As we have seen, David and the psalmists experienced moments of person-to-Person prayer as communion and encounter with God. However, the psalmists expressed in ritual practice and poetic form what Jeremiah experienced in his personal encounters with God.

With Jeremiah prayer was an overwhelming passion, sustained, intimate, personal, and creative. Moreover, we have detailed knowledge of his inner life that provides greater insight into the depths of his personal relationship with God. No one can read chapters 11-20 and 23 of the book of Jeremiah without being aware of his profound experiences in the deeper dimensions of prayer.

So what was it that defined Jeremiah's pioneer work on prayer? From Jeremiah's encounters with God in prayer, we can gain three basic insights.

Prayer as Intimate Conversation with God

Jeremiah communicated through his writings that prayer is an intimately personal conversation with God. In the book of Jeremiah there was directness in this divine-human relationship that opened up new avenues of prayer for all succeeding generations. From the very first chapter of Jeremiah, we hear an open and honest dialogue between Jeremiah and God in which Jeremiah acknowledges who God is and even tries to argue what God is not.

> *The word of the Lord came to me saying, "Before I formed you in the womb I knew you, before you were born I set you apart; I appointed you as a prophet to the nations." "Ah, Sovereign Lord," I said, "I do not know how to speak; I am only a child." But the Lord said to me, "Do not say, 'I am only a child.' You must go to everyone I send you to and say whatever I command you. Do not be afraid of them, for I am with you and will rescue you," declares the Lord.*
> **Jeremiah 1:4-8 NIV**

Among those who expressed the spirit of this kind of prayer were the psalmists who, along with Jeremiah, have taught those in the Judeo-Christian heritage what it means to pray in a deeply personal and intimate way.

Prayer Rooted in the Struggles of Life

Second, like the psalmists, Jeremiah revealed that prayer, at its best, finds us in the profoundest struggles of life in which we reveal our true hearts to God. According to Jeremiah, God puts the righteous to the test and makes known his opposition to wickedness.

O Lord of hosts, you test the righteous, you see the heart and the mind; let me see your retribution upon them, for to you I have committed my cause.

Jeremiah 20:12 NRSV

We have seen that prayer is person-to-Person communion and a personal encounter with God. But this sounds like a pale abstraction compared to the desperate struggles of Jeremiah in his own encounters with the Almighty. God met Jeremiah where he was, in the heart of life, in the center of personal and community issues and struggles. The people had corrupted their religion by turning to other gods and to pagan ways. Having forgotten God's covenant, they were substituting a cheap and easy ritualism at the Temple for right living before God. Even the priests and prophets had abandoned the faith to pursue their godless ways. In response to the corruption all around him, Jeremiah was engaged in a continual message from God to call the people to repentance and to change their hearts.

*Jeremiah, say to the people, "This is what the L*ORD *says: When people fall down, don't they get up again? When they start down the wrong road and discover their mistake, don't they turn back?*

Then why do these people keep going along their self-destructive path, refusing to turn back, even though I have warned them?

I listen to their conversations, and what do I hear? Is anyone sorry for sin? Does anyone say, 'What a terrible thing I have done'? No! All are running down the path of sin as swiftly as a horse rushing into battle!

The stork knows the time of her migration, as do the turtledove, the swallow, and the crane. They all return at the *proper time each year. But not my people! They do not know what the L*ORD *requires of them."*

Jeremiah 8:4-7 NLT

Besides the internal corruption of the people and their leaders, there was the threat of domination from foreign nations. And eventually, during Jeremiah's lifetime and in keeping with his unpopular predictions, Jerusalem fell to the Babylonians. The towns of Judah were destroyed and the people were taken into captivity.

In the context of these actual and impending spiritual and political disasters, Jeremiah pours out his soul to God. Loneliness, grief, and despair are clearly articulated in his personal conversations with God. However, these intimate conversations with God did not make his relationship or call easy. Indeed, he deplores the fact that he was born and curses the day of his birth.

What sadness is mine, my mother. Oh, that I had died at birth!

Jeremiah 15:10 NLT

Overwhelmed with loneliness, Jeremiah cries to God:

I did not sit in the company of merrymakers, nor did I rejoice; under the weight of your hand I sat alone, for you had filled me with indignation.

Jeremiah 15:17 NRSV

Jeremiah pours out his bitterness toward Almighty God when he prays:

O Lord, you deceived me, and I was deceived; you overpowered me and prevailed. I am ridiculed all day long; everyone mocks me.

Jeremiah 20:7 NIV

In his anguish, Jeremiah reminds us that prayer as a personal conversation with God at times requires honest and even raw emotions where we express our frustration with God of our circumstances.

The word *existentialism* means to focus on a person's inner struggles, decisions, anxieties, loneliness, alienation, doubt and despair. Jeremiah enters into the depths of existential passion in prayer. And this kind of continual trial is an inherent feature of prayer in the biblical heritage. For no one can be in the presence of God and ignore the agonizing struggles of humanity.

Personal conversation with God at times requires honest, even raw, emotions.

Prayer as Light in the Darkness

Third, Jeremiah taught us that no matter how dark the night, God's day is sure to come if we will return. Apart from God there is no hope. So God spoke to Jeremiah, saying:

> *Cursed are those who put their trust in mere humans and turn their hearts away from the Lord.*
>
> **Jeremiah 17:5 NLT**

But the one who trusts in the Lord is like a tree that remains green and bears fruit despite the surrounding drought (17:8). Jeremiah's vision of God's new day comes to historic significance when he speaks of the glorious new covenant:

"The days are surely coming," says the Lord, "when I will make a new covenant with the house of Israel and the house of Judah. "

"But this is the covenant that I will make with the house of Israel after those days," says the Lord. "I will put my law within them, and I will write it on their hearts; and I will be their God, and they shall be my people."

Jeremiah 31:31, 33 NRSV

Great as he was, Jeremiah left something to be desired in his prayer-life. He lacked the psalmists' sense of gratitude and thanksgiving, and he carried the spirit of vengeance too much with him when he prayed:

You know they plan to kill me. So get angry and punish them! Don't ever forgive their terrible crimes.

Jeremiah 18:23 CEV

This is another reminder that in the biblical understanding of prayer the Old Testament prepares the way for the teaching and example of Jesus and the apostles. Much that the psalmists and prophets taught on prayer abides in its own right. Their inspired writings have ageless glory. In addition, they reveal the glory of preparing the way for what was yet to come in the promised coming of our Savior.

Through prayer, God brings the promise of Light into our darkness.

Questions for Reflection

1. Jeremiah, like many of the prophets, had the privilege of having an actual conversation or dialogue with God. When have you had the experience of having a personal and intimate conversation with God? What made it personal and conversational?

2. Jeremiah passionately poured out his heart to God expressing the heights of joy and the depths of despair. When and how have you been honest and open with your emotions in your prayers to God?

3. Despite all the despair, Jeremiah also saw Light in the darkness through his conversations with God. When has God revealed promise and light to you in prayer during times of darkness and despair?

person-to-Person Connection

Conversation that honors relationship allows both parties to speak and to listen to the other. Set aside time each day where you read God's Word and allow God to speak to you in the midst of your circumstances before responding to God in prayer.

Five

Paul on Prayer

Next to Jesus, Paul was the greatest teacher on prayer that the world has seen. He taught the congregations he formed to be praying communities-so much so, in fact, that he could be called the creator of Christian congregational prayer. He helped people to avoid the pitfalls of an artificial prayer-life by emphasizing the permanent, sustaining factors in authentic prayer.

What are those emphases, which Paul taught by precept and example, that have guided the community of prayer, faith, and service throughout the centuries? Paul shared with us four things that have a permanent place in the Christian practice of prayer.

Christ-centered Prayer

First, Paul taught that our fellowship with God is directly related to the central place of Jesus Christ in our faith. There is a curious mixture of mystery and insight here. We do not know in human terms why, when we meditate on what Jesus said and did and decide to follow him, we feel ourselves mysteriously drawn to God. We only know that this is so. But this is not merely a human discovery: It is a divine revelation. Our communion with God through Jesus Christ moves from the more mystical and abstract sense of the divine Presence toward the intimately personal awareness of the loving Father.

In Paul, this Christ-centeredness in prayer was inevitable because Paul's new life as a whole revolved around Jesus Christ. He did not find in his Hebrew heritage what he most wanted. To be sure, he was inspired by Abraham, Moses, the prophets, and the psalmists. But he understood them to be chosen by God to prepare the way for moving from the law to grace. So his supreme source of the new life came from Christ alone.

How did it happen that this Pharisee of the Pharisees (who was determined to outrun his peers) should focus on Jesus Christ as the supreme source of spiritual power? Perhaps he saw a level of spiritual victory in the Christians whom he had been persecuting. And surely he saw this in Stephen, who prayed for those who were killing him. So Saul, this determined, persistent, spiritual athlete, now saw a new realm of possibility for his soul. Paul also experienced an awful inner conflict which was mercifully resolved when the Risen Lord confronted him personally on the road to Damascus. Therefore, when Paul talked, preached, or wrote about prayer, it was always Christ-centered. For through Christ alone, he knew himself to be a "new creation." Through Christ alone, he was lifted into the new dimension of existence as a Christian.

No wonder he spoke of Jesus as being the very center of faith when he said:

> *But we proclaim Christ crucified... but to those who are called, both Jews and Greeks, Christ the power of God and the wisdom of God.*
> **First Corinthians 1:23-24 NRSV**

Paul likewise proclaimed that Jesus was the lens through which he regarded all else: *for I decided to concentrate only on*

Jesus Christ. (First Corinthians 2:2 NLT). Even further, Paul declared that his life was meaningless apart from Jesus Christ.

> **I have been crucified with Christ and I no longer live, but Christ lives in me.**
>
> **Galatians 2:20 NIV**

It is not surprising that the man who spoke this out of the deepest recesses of his own spirituality should have made Christ central in his prayer-life. When he thanked God, he did so *through Jesus Christ* (Romans 1:8). When he asked others to give thanks in all circumstances, it was because *this is the will of God in Christ Jesus for you* (First Thessalonians 5:18). Paul remembered the Christians at Ephesus in his prayers and prayed that *the God of our Lord Jesus Christ, the Father of glory,* might give them a spirit of wisdom and of revelation in the knowledge of Christ (Ephesians 1:16-17). It is almost impossible to exaggerate the creative power of Christ in the prayer-life of Paul. Everything centers in Christ. Everything flows from God through Jesus. And in prayer, the divine grace transforms through Christ.

We are to be thankful not necessarily for all circumstances but in all circumstances.

In All Things, Give Thanks

This brings us to the second major emphasis Paul made in his teaching on prayer. He, more than anyone else except Jesus, insisted that gratitude or thanksgiving is essential in all true Christian prayer. Indeed for Paul, gratitude to God was a permanent feature of a healthy Christian life. And in prayer, thanksgiving was poured out to God as an essential feature of the devout life.

As we have seen, Paul said that we should give thanks in all circumstances. This means that in sickness or health, in tragedy or triumph, in sorrow or joy, we should give thanks to God. Then, as if to show that this is no merely whimsical utterance, he reminds us why we should do so.

> *Give thanks in all circumstances, for this is God's will for you in Christ Jesus.*
>
> **First Thessalonians 5:18 NIV**

Paul is not suggesting that we should be thankful for bad circumstances. Rather, that we should be thankful in all circumstances.

Paul did truly give thanks in all sorts of times and circumstances. He gave thanks to God when he wrote to the Christians in Rome because their faith *is proclaimed throughout the world.* (Romans 1:8) He was filled with gratitude because of the supernatural deliverance from sin: *Thanks be to God through Jesus Christ our Lord!* (Romans 7:25) He urged the Ephesians to give thanks when he said:

> *Be filled with the Spirit, as you sing psalms and hymns and spiritual songs among yourselves, singing and making melody to the Lord in your hearts, giving thanks to God the Father at all times and for everything in the name of our Lord Jesus Christ.*
>
> **Ephesians 5:18-20 NRSV**

And in his prayers for the Philippians, Paul expressed his gratitude to God for their partnership with him in the Gospel.

I thank my God every time I remember you. In all my prayers for all of you, I always pray with joy because of your partnership in the gospel from the first day until now....
Philippians 1:3-5 NIV

Despite difficult circumstances he urged them to *rejoice in the Lord.* (3:1) Again and again, by precept and example, Paul called upon the Christians to rejoice and give thanks in their prayers.

Do not worry about anything, but in everything by prayer and supplication with thanksgiving let your requests be made known to God.
Philippians 4:6 NRSV

Stand in the Gap for Others

Paul also brought a third major emphasis which has a permanent place in Christian prayer. Just as Paul guided the early Christian congregations in expressing gratitude, so Paul shaped the church's mind on intercessory prayer or praying intently for others. He practiced it and taught it with a passion. As Heiler says,

Paul has put intercessory prayer at the very centre of the devotional life of the Christian. He himself, the great missionary and pastor, was a master of the art of intercessory prayer.

Paul prayed without growing weary for the people in the churches he established. And to those in Rome—whose church he did not establish—he wrote:

God knows how often I pray for you. Day and night I bring you and your needs in prayer to God.
Romans 1:9 NLT

He likewise prayed continuously for the Christians at Corinth (First Corinthians 1:4-8; Second Corinthians 13:7-9), and he prayed for those at Ephesus (Ephesians 1:15-17). He prayed for the church at Philippi (Philippians 1:3-5), and he prayed for the believers in Thessalonica (First Thessalonians 1:23). Paul also prayed for the individuals like Philemon, Apphia, and Archippus (Philemon 2-4).

And, of course, Paul asked other Christians to pray for him as they prayed for each other. For despite all of his extraordinary experiences and abilities, he felt profoundly the need for the prayers of Christians in the churches.

> *My friends, by the power of the Lord Jesus Christ and by the love that comes from the Holy Spirit, I beg you to pray sincerely with me and for me. Pray that God will protect me from the unbelievers in Judea, and that his people in Jerusalem will be pleased with what I am doing. Ask God to let me come to you and have a pleasant and refreshing visit.*
> **Romans 15:30-32 CEV**

Pray without Ceasing

One more emphasis which Paul brought in his teaching on prayer is that of constancy. No merely sporadic efforts will be adequate to the need. There is doubtless a place for those sudden ventures into prayer which come out of the depths of tragedy. But, as Paul saw, these are not the norm for most of our Christian experience. Most of our lives are marked less by trauma and more by the daily ebb and flow of life's demands. In the face of these daily demands, Paul invited people to be constant in prayer and thus to practice prayer as a habit of Christian living. He said to the Romans, *Rejoice in your hope, be patient in suffering, persevere in prayer* (Romans 12:12). He asked the Ephesians to *pray in the Spirit at all times* (Ephesians 6:18). He urged the Thessalonians to *pray without ceasing* (First Thessalonians 5:17). And he called the Colossians to *devote themselves to prayer, keeping alert in it with thanksgiving* (Colossians 4:2-3 NRSV).

We hear much these days about life-styles, and even the Christian life has been at times classified as a life-style. However, this suggests that Christianity is just a fashion among other ways of living. This kind of thinking is far removed from Paul's undersstanding of what it means to be a Christian. To Paul, steadfastness in prayer was like food and breathing, a daily necessity which cannot be forgotten or avoided. For a Christian is to be a person of prayer and faith who, not conforming to the paltry standards of this world, lives under the sway of Jesus Christ. Thus, as Christians, prayer, constant and Christ-centered, is essential to our daily living. Without it, our life in Christ cannot be sustained.

To Paul, steadfastness in prayer is like food and breathing–a daily necessity.

Questions for Reflection

1. Paul's prayer-life was remarkably Christ-centered. We often say in our prayers, "In Christ's name we pray." In what ways could you more specifically and powerfully pray not only proclaiming Jesus at the end of your prayers but praying Jesus at the center of your prayers?

2. Paul reminds us to give thanks in all times and circumstances–what the Psalmist might also call a "sacrifice of praise." What is the difference in giving thanks "in" all circumstances as opposed to "for" all circumstances?

3. For Paul, prayer was like eating or breathing–an essential part of daily life. How would your prayer life be different if it were more like rhythmic "breathing" instead of a sudden one-time gasp?

person–to–Person connection

For Paul, intercessory prayer was not simply a "laundry list" of praying for people in need. Even more so, it involved thinking on and giving thanks for the people for whom he was praying.

Think of an individual who is standing in need of your prayers. Begin to think (and possibly journal) about them and their particular needs and how God may regard them and their needs. Give God thanks for them and give thanks in advance for the mighty ways you expect God to move in their lives.

Six

Jesus on Prayer

Before considering some specific teachings of Jesus on prayer, we need to lift up two basic facts. The first is that Jesus prayed. The second is that his example as the essence and heart of prayer had a powerful influence on his disciples.

Jesus prayed.

I am not saying that a Jewish peasant prayed, or that an unusually charismatic individual prayed. I am emphasizing that Jesus Christ, the Son of God and Savior of the world, prayed. He who is the Way, the Truth, and the Life began and continued his mission with prayer. He commanded his followers to pray. And what he taught with his lips he demonstrated in his life.

> *After he had dismissed them, he went up on a mountainside by himself to pray.*
> **Matthew 14:23 NIV**

> *Then Jesus brought them to an olive grove called Gethsemane, and he said, "Sit here while I go on ahead to pray." He took Peter and Zebedee's two sons, James and John, and he began to be filled with anguish and deep distress. He told them, "My soul is crushed with grief to the point of death. Stay here and watch with me." He went on a little farther and fell face down on the ground, praying, "My Father! If it is possible, let this cup of suffering be taken*

away from me. Yet I want your will, not mine." Then he returned to the disciples and found them asleep. He said to Peter, "Couldn't you stay awake and watch with me even one hour? Keep alert and pray. Otherwise temptation will overpower you. For though the spirit is willing enough, the body is weak!" Again he left them and prayed, "My Father! If this cup cannot be taken away until I drink it, your will be done." He returned to them again and found them sleeping, for they just couldn't keep their eyes open.

So he went back to pray a third time, saying the same things again.

Matthew 26:36-44 NLT

Now in the morning, having risen a long while before daylight, He went out and departed to a solitary place; and there He prayed.

Mark 1:35 NKJV

After saying farewell to them, he went up on the mountain to pray.

Mark 6:46 NRSV

While everyone else was being baptized, Jesus himself was baptized. Then as he prayed, the sky opened up...

Luke 3:21 CEV

But he would withdraw to deserted places and pray.

Luke 5:16 NRSV

One day as Jesus was alone, praying, he came over to his disciples and asked them, "Who do people say I am?"
About eight days later Jesus took Peter, James, and John to a mountain to pray. And as he was praying, the appearance of his face changed, and his clothing became dazzling white.

Luke 9:18, 28-29 NLT

But I have prayed for you that your own faith may not fail;

*and you, when once you have turned back, strengthen your
brothers.
Then he withdrew from them about a stone's throw, knelt
down, and prayed.
In his anguish he prayed more earnestly, and his sweat
became like great drops of blood falling down on the ground.*
                                        Luke 22:32, 41, 44 NRSV

The development of a complete person-to-Person prayer
life, for which the Old Testament prepared the way, reached
its highest expression in Jesus. The fact that he prayed is of
utmost importance in leading us into the life of prayer. As we
have seen in the Old Testament, some of the psalmists and
Jeremiah attain a high level of prayer as personal communion
and encounter with God. But Jesus is the Master teacher on
prayer.

What Jesus taught about prayer is most clearly seen in the
quality and influence of his example as the essence and heart
of prayer. The disciples of Jesus felt this profoundly.

Communion with the Father

Early in his ministry, Jesus called the disciples to be his
helpers in his special mission in the Kingdom of God.
This means that they were brought into intimate personal
relationship with Jesus. They ate with him. They listened
to him. They asked him questions within the privacy of
their group. They could observe him in his work as Teacher,
Physician, and Preacher. No one else had this privilege. They
alone had the firsthand knowledge of Jesus as embodying
the soul of prayer. The disciples had seen Jesus praying. They
doubtless overheard him many times when he prayed.

They knew by direct experience that there was something different about his prayer life from that of the Pharisees and other religious leaders. They knew that Jesus and the Heavenly Father were on the most intimate of terms. And they wanted to experience for themselves something of that same communion with the Father.

In Luke's Gospel we read about the disciples asking Jesus to teach them how to pray. They had been watching Jesus praying and asked for help. He responded,

When you pray, say:
Father, hallowed be your name, your kingdom come.
Give us each day our daily bread.
Forgive us our sins,
for we also forgive everyone who sins against us.
And lead us not into temptation.

Luke 11:1-4 NIV

The twelve disciples knew that Jesus prayed and also that he alone could give them the guidance they needed for their own prayer life. By his example, Jesus was for them the Master-teacher on prayer. Therefore, regarding prayer, they looked beyond the patriarchs, beyond the psalmists, and beyond the prophets to Jesus. In all of this, the apostles have guided Christians throughout the centuries. And they have taught us to look to Jesus as our final guide in our own prayer life.

Jesus embodied the Soul of Prayer as communion with the Father.

Prayer-shaped Life

The whole life of Jesus might be described as an extended life of prayer. Although he did not spend all his time in prayer, his life was shaped and guided by prayer. His parables and other teachings tell us of the wide ranges of his observations on human life. He thought, spoke and acted on many things. He spoke of seed and soil and sowing and harvest. He reflected on mothers and fathers and children–on young and old, male and female, rich and poor, weak and strong. He knew from direct observation the peril of the love of riches. And, by virtue of his continuing experiences with both friends and enemies, he knew what was in human beings. In the thick of life in community, he carried out his mission. He laughed and wept. He healed the sick. He preached and taught. And he suffered and died for the sins of the world.

Through Jesus' prayer at Gethsemane, an obscure garden became a hallowed spot in Christian history.

Somehow, amid all of his many thoughts, observations, and deeds, everything he did seems to have flowed from him as the supreme Soul of prayer. And when we behold him on the Cross, we know that what happened there came out of his prayer in that garden of agony. By the work of his prayer at Gethsemane, everything was changed until an otherwise obscure garden became a hallowed spot in Christian history. It was because of the Master's supreme moment of prayer in that place. It was there, more than anywhere else, that Jesus taught us to put our absolute trust in God even in the midst of our most desperate circumstances. His triumph in prayer at Gethsemane and Calvary teaches us that God's redemptive mission throughout the whole world must go on at all cost. Jesus had his cross to bear, and, as we pray and work in the Kingdom, we know that we too must deny ourselves and take up our cross and follow him.

Jesus taught us the unspeakable beauty and glory of a life of prayer which ushers in deeds of sheer courage and total dedication to God. He demonstrated what can happen when we return again and again to God in prayer until all else that we do receives its motivation and power from God as the source of all life.

Prayer as Personal Understanding

By example, as well as precept, Jesus taught us also that his own prayer life came from his understanding of God and human beings. It is beyond question that Jesus' approach to prayer was based on his understanding of God as Father. If we think of God merely as a Cosmic Process, we cannot enter into a person-to-Person prayer life. We cannot pray to a process, whether cosmic or not. If we believe that God is a vague impersonal Being-in-itself, prayer is almost sure to be reduced to meditation and aspiration. But, with Jesus, God *is* personal. God knows us, loves us, cares for us and responds to us. So, inevitably, there is with Jesus this sense of the most intimate interpersonal relationship with God. This is doubtless one reason why he deliberately taught his disciples to begin their prayer with the words, "Our

Father." Yet Jesus did not in the least reduce the sense of the greatness and glory of God. Therefore, he taught his disciples to pray, *Our Father, who art in heaven, Hallowed be Thy name.*

The category of sex has no assignable meaning in relation to God.

An Understanding of Father God

Jesus was the only founder of a world religion to teach his followers to pray to God as Father. He was not teaching them to think of God in terms of maleness. For he knew God to be a Spirit who is neither male nor female. We may throw some light on this matter of God and sexuality by two brief comments. The first is that there is in the English language no pronoun which transcends or rises above the male and female genders. To speak of God as "it" would be to reduce God to an impersonal term which is inconsistent with the biblical revelation. The second comment is that we get the best insight into who God is through what we experience as our own personhood, or mind, or soul. To use the last term, our souls are neither male nor female. And the qualities which define our nature as souls are those which enable us to gain some understanding of the personal God revealed in the Bible. To be sure, the qualities by which we identify ourselves (consciousness, selfhood, self-identity, knowledge, purpose, volition, or choices we make as well as love and the power to communicate) are finite and radically limited. But they provide the best clues we have to understanding the personal God in whom Jesus taught us to believe. And these categories are neither male nor female. The category of sex has no assignable meaning in relation to God.

The combination of the infinite greatness of God and of God's marvelous approachability guided the disciples of Jesus in their prayer-life. And the understanding of God as Father has informed the prayers of the continuing community of faith throughout the centuries. So when others pray to God as Father, we should remind ourselves of the absolute immeasurable nature of God. And though prayer is a dynamic source of creative energy, it is always communion and encounter with God. It is both an end-in-itself and a divinely appointed means of doing God's work.

What Jesus Teaches about Prayer

In instructing the disciples, Jesus teaches us seven things about prayer.

Brevity in Prayer

First, he taught us to be brief, to come to the point and to be specific. He taught us to pray for forgiveness and for the power to carry out God's holy purpose. He taught us also to pray for daily bread and for victory over temptation. Physical and spiritual needs were joined together with sublime brevity in our Lord's Prayer. The effect of this teaching is to keep us away from pompous, ostentatious, and unnatural language in prayer.

> *When you pray, don't babble on and on as people of other religions do. They think their prayers are answered only by repeating their words again and again.*
>
> **Matthew 6:7 NLT**

Now, please note: Brevity was the general rule. But we know, of course, that at times Jesus could not be brief because he continued all night in prayer for special purposes. And in the Garden of Gethsemane, he agonized in prayer far longer than a few brief moments.

Pray by Faith

Second, Jesus taught us to pray in faith and to expect results. He said:

> *Ask and it will be given to you; seek and you will find; knock and the door will be opened to you.*
>
> **Matthew 7:7 NIV**

When he said, "Ask," he did not mean "make a casual request." When he said, "Search," he did not mean "look around a little." And when he said, "Knock," he did not mean "tap on the door lightly." The words ask, seek, and knock are strong words. They suggest that in prayer we must be bold, passionate, and earnest. They suggest also that we must pray in faith, knowing that God wants to bless us. For, as Jesus said:

> *If you sinful people know how to give good gifts to your children, how much more will your heavenly Father give good gifts to those who ask him.*
>
> **Matthew 7:11 NLT**

The words "how much more" are crucial. An imperfect parent wants to do good things for the children. How much more does the Father who is perfect and holy want to bless us! Therefore, we are to pray in faith and expect God's blessings.

Persistence in Prayer

Jesus taught us to be persistent in prayer. This thought builds on the preceding one. Here the mind of the Master meets the best insights of psychology by weaving into the life of prayer the principle of a sustained desire. God responds graciously to those who, in keeping with the divine purpose, let their desires come to focus in their prayers. This promise of blessings found in Matthew 5:6 is particularly true of those who hunger and thirst for righteousness, for they shall be satisfied. And in Matthew 6:33 we see that those who seek first the Kingdom of God and his righteousness will receive many other blessings. Prayer and losing heart do not mix. The Master illustrated this graphically in his parable of the widow's persistence before the unrighteous judge.

> *Jesus told his disciples a story about how they should keep on praying and never give up: In a town there was once a judge who didn't fear God or care about people. In that same town there was a widow who kept going to the judge and saying, "Make sure that I get fair treatment in court."*
>
> *For a while the judge refused to do anything. Finally, he said to himself, "Even though I don't fear God or care about people, I will help this widow because she keeps on bothering me. If I don't help her, she will wear me out."*
>
> *The Lord said: "Think about what that crooked judge said. Won't God protect his chosen ones who pray to him day and night? Won't he be concerned for them? He will surely hurry and help them. But when the Son of Man comes, will he find on this earth anyone with faith?"*
>
> **Luke 18:1-8 CEV**

Honesty

Jesus taught that basic honesty is an indispensable condition for true prayer. He wanted us to be honest enough not to hide our sins and frailties under a mask of forms and ceremonies. So he said:

> *If you remain in me and my words remain in you, ask whatever you wish, and it will be given you. This is to my Father's glory, that you bear much fruit, showing yourselves to be my disciples.*
>
> **John 15:7-8 NIV**

The parable of the two men praying in the temple can remind us of our own attempts at prayer.

> *Then Jesus told this story to some who had great self-confidence and scorned everyone else: "Two men went to the Temple to pray. One was a Pharisee, and the other was a dishonest tax collector. The proud Pharisee stood by himself and prayed this prayer: 'I thank you, God, that I am not a sinner like everyone else, especially like that tax collector over there! For I never cheat, I don't sin, I don't commit adultery, I fast twice a week, and I give you a tenth of my income.'*
>
> *"But the tax collector stood at a distance and dared not even lift his eyes to heaven as he prayed. Instead, he beat his chest in sorrow, saying, 'O God, be merciful to me, for I am a sinner.' I tell you, this sinner, not the Pharisee, returned home justified before God. For the proud will be humbled, but the humble will be honored."*
>
> **Luke 18:9-14 NLT**

The Master knew that everyone could be aware of a basic rightness or wrongness with God. And he knew that the only way to approach God is in the spirit of honesty, sincerity, and consequently the willingness to obey. This is why Jesus taught his followers to pray in his name:

> *You can ask for anything in my name, and I will do it,*
> *because the work of the Son brings glory to the Father.*
>
> **John 14:13**

> *You didn't choose me. I chose you. I appointed you to go and*
> *produce fruit that will last, so that the Father will give you*
> *whatever you ask for, using my name.*
>
> **John 15:16**

> *At that time you won't need to ask me for anything. The*
> *truth is, you can go directly to the Father and ask him, and*
> *he will grant your request because you use my name.*
>
> **John 16:23**

For when we pray in the name of Jesus, we are filled with his spirit and seek what he wants. In this way our prayers will rise to God out of the inward flow of the love of Christ.

Not All About Me

Fifth, Jesus taught his followers to pray for each other and for the needs of the whole world. This is seen in his call to pray:

> *When he saw the crowds, he had compassion for them,*
> *because they were harassed and helpless, like sheep without a*
> *shepherd.*
>
> *Then he said to his disciples, "The harvest is plentiful, but*
> *the laborers are few; therefore ask the Lord of the harvest to*
> *send out laborers into his harvest."*
>
> **Matthew 9:36-39 NRSV**

This spirit of intercession is implied also in the Master's repeated instructions on forgiving others:

> *But when you are praying, first forgive anyone you are*

holding a grudge against, so that your Father in heaven will forgive your sins, too.

Mark 11:25 NLT

Through prayer and fasting we can do great things for others. The powers of evil, both within and without, are often defeated by the earnest prayers of the faithful. Jesus prayed for Peter, that he might be delivered from the power of Satan. He said:

Simon, Simon, Satan has asked to sift you as wheat. But I have prayed for you, Simon, that your faith may not fail. And when you have turned back, strengthen your brothers.

Luke 22:31-32 NIV

All of the Master's teaching on praying for others was brought to a magnificent summation in his own great prayer for his followers found in John 17.

When Jesus had finished saying all these things, he looked up to heaven and said, "Father, the time has come. Glorify your Son so he can give glory back to you. For you have given him authority over everyone in all the earth. He gives eternal life to each one you have given him. And this is the way to have eternal life—to know you, the only true God, and Jesus Christ, the one you sent to earth. I brought glory to you here on earth by doing everything you told me to do. And now, Father, bring me into the glory we shared before the world began.

I have told these men about you. They were in the world, but then you gave them to me. Actually, they were always yours, and you gave them to me; and they have kept your word. Now they know that everything I have is a gift from you, for I have passed on to them the words you gave me; and they accepted them and know that I came from you, and they believe you sent me. My prayer is not for the world, but for those you have given me, because they belong to you. And all of them, since they are mine, belong to you; and you have given them back to me, so they are my glory!

Now I am departing the world; I am leaving them behind and coming to you. Holy Father, keep them and care for them—all those you have given me—so that they will be united just as we are. During my time here, I have kept them safe. I guarded them so that not one was lost, except the one headed for destruction, as the Scriptures foretold. "And now I am coming to you. I have told them many things while I was with them so they would be filled with my joy. I have given them your word. And the world hates them because they do not belong to the world, just as I do not. I'm not asking you to take them out of the world, but to keep them safe from the evil one. They are not part of this world any more than I am.

Make them pure and holy by teaching them your words of truth. As you sent me into the world, I am sending them into the world. And I give myself entirely to you so they also might be entirely yours.

I am praying not only for these disciples but also for all who will ever believe in me because of their testimony. My prayer for all of them is that they will be one, just as you and I are one, Father—that just as you are in me and I am in you, so they will be in us, and the world will believe you sent me. I have given them the glory you gave me, so that they may be one, as we are—I in them and you in me, all being perfected into one. Then the world will know that you sent me and will understand that you love them as much as you love me.

Father, I want these whom you've given me to be with me,

so they can see my glory. You gave me the glory because you loved me even before the world began! O righteous Father, the world doesn't know you, but I do; and these disciples know you sent me. And I have revealed you to them and will keep on revealing you. I will do this so that your love for me may be in them and I in them."

John 17 NLT

He carried this further when he included us, too. For he said:
I do not pray for these only, but also for those who are to believe in me through their word, that they may all be one....

John 17:20-21 RSV

We may have our doubts about praying for others, but Jesus did not. Christians throughout the centuries have practiced the habit of praying for others, and God has blessed them with abundant harvests.

Give Thanks

Sixth, Jesus taught us to express thanksgiving in prayer. When the seventy-two returned with joy from their mission as evangelists, Jesus prayed:
I praise you, Father, Lord of heaven and earth, because you have hidden these things from the wise and learned, and revealed them to little children. Yes, Father, for this was your good pleasure.

Luke 10:21 NIV

And before the tomb of Lazarus he prayed:
After the stone had been rolled aside, Jesus looked up toward heaven and prayed, "Father, I thank you for answering my prayer."

John 11:41 CEV

It was no accident that Paul, who was determined to imitate Jesus, became the great champion of gratitude as an essential characteristic of the Christian. Through Jesus, the practice of being thankful to God became a basic principle of the devotional life.

Giving Glory to God

Seventh, Jesus taught that the supreme purpose of prayer is to glorify God and to strive with God in the work of the Kingdom. We cannot emphasize too much God's holy purpose for all human beings: God wants us to respond to divine love, to receive the proffered grace and blessings, and to weave into our passing earthly lives God's holy concerns. In this, Jesus was our perfect example. He made it his habit to go apart for prayer before his major decisions. We can see Jesus spending time in prayer before entering upon his public ministry. (Look in Matthew 4, Mark 1, and Luke 4 for this pattern of behavior.) He was led by the Spirit into the wilderness to pray. He went out to a mountain to pray–and continued all night in prayer–before making his final selection of the twelve disciples from among his followers:

> *Now during those days he went out to the mountain to pray; and he spent the night in prayer to God. And when day came, he called his disciples and chose twelve of them, whom he also named apostles.*
>
> **Luke 6:12-16 NRSV**

The greatest sentence ever uttered in a prayer is this one said by Jesus in Matthew 6:10:

> *Thy kingdom come.*
> *Thy will be done on earth, as it is in heaven.*

Jesus wanted to remind us that our prayers are about God, about what God is doing, and about what God will be doing. If we do not pray this prayer, we need not pray any other. It is the foundation on which all Christian prayers are built. Jesus demonstrated his commitment to God's holy purpose during his agonizing prayer at Gethsemane found in Luke 22 when, after his appeals to God, he submitted to God's will over his own.

The Religion of the Heart of Jesus

William Hazlitt is one of my favorite authors. However, as far as I know, he wrote nothing about Jesus other than this:

His was the religion of the heart. We see it in his discourse with the Disciples as they walked together toward Emmaus, when their hearts burned within them; in his sermon from the Mount, in his parable of the Good Samaritan, and in that of the Prodigal Son–in every act and word of his life, a grace, a mildness, a dignity and love, a patience and wisdom worthy of the Son of God. His whole life and being were imbued, steeped in this word, *charity;* it was the spring, the well-head from which every thought and feeling gushed into act; and it was this that breathed a mild glory from his face in that last agony upon the cross, "when the meek Savior bowed his head and died," praying for his enemies. He was the first true teacher of morality; for he alone conceived the idea of a pure humanity....

He taught the love of good for the sake of good, without regard to personal or sinister views, and made the affections of the heart the sole seat of morality....

The very idea of abstract benevolence, of the desire to do good because another wants our services, and of regarding the human race as one family, the offspring of one common parent, is hardly to be found in any other code or system....

But in the Christian relition we perceive a softness coming over the heart of a nation, and the iron scales that fence and harden it, melt and drop off.

As the Master Teacher in the life of prayer, Jesus Christ abides through all generations. For in this too, he is the same yesterday and today and for ever (Hebrews 13:8). There are huge gala spectacles throughout the world where vast multitudes come together to hear popular music, to witness athletic events, and to participate in political conventions. In the light of these and the countless other distractions which capture the people's attention, we sometimes feel that Jesus Christ and his call to prayer are lost in the tumult and the shouting.

But long after these spectacles and diversions have tumbled down the currents of history and flowed into the vast ocean of oblivion, the imperial glory of the life of Christ will continue to capture young people everywhere and command the allegiance of people of all ages. His mighty act of redemption on the cross abides, forever. And his life of prayer will guide people throughout the world as they choose to join each other in the ageless pilgrimage with God.

Questions for Reflection

1. Prayer converted the obscure garden of Gethsemane into a holy place in history. What place or time becomes holy for you through prayer?

2. Jesus reminds us that our prayers are to be about God— about who God is and what God does. What changes would you make in your prayers for them to be less about you and more about God?

3. Jesus taught and embodied persistence in prayer. When have you experienced persistence in prayer producing results?

person-to-Person connection

Think of one particular focus in your prayer life that has required persistence. Envision that you are standing at God's door in prayer.

*   Ask God boldly for what is needed.
*   Search for God's will in the matter by opening your heart to dialogue with God.
*   Knock continually on the door of God's heart until it is opened and answered.

Seven

Prayer and Our Thoughts

Now that we have explored the biblical foundation for our prayers, we must also acknowledge that there are also obstacles to our prayer-life. In the next several chapters we will explore some profound problems and hungers which are satisfied by God's grace through prayer.

It is easy to see obvious mistakes. Everyone knows when a baseball player makes an error. Everyone can see when a juggler misses the act. And everyone knows the obvious enemies of God and prayer. We do not require special instruction to see that alcoholism, drug addiction, lying, stealing, cursing, greed, lust, disloyalty, violence and other actions impede our relationship with God in prayer.

But many things take place within us which are almost too close to see. In fact, they are so close, they take place in our minds. For instance, our ever-flowing streams of consciousness move from thought to thought and experience to experience. During every waking moment we are thinking of something. And often in our sleep, things flow into our minds apparently without much rhyme or reason. Most of our thoughts, day or night, come in and pass away. They are soon lost in the vast oblivion of forgotten things. This stream of consciousness in each of us, which continues to flow through our simply being as persons, is characteristic of our human nature. To ask people to stop this flow of constant thought is to ask them to stop living. Therefore, the walk with God, the practice of prayer, must take place within souls which experience this continual inner flow of thoughts.

In the light of this bedrock fact about ourselves, we can understand why so much effort is placed on thought-control, self-understanding, and disciplined living. Socrates gave the world something important when he said: *Know thyself.* Jesus stated that it is critically important to save our souls by losing them in devotion to God and others. These and countless other teachings and maxims focus on the organization and control of our thoughts. Therefore, our thoughts have an ageless relevance.

So, what is it that makes us who we are? At least three things: our thoughts, desires, and emotions. These three are mysteriously interwoven to form strangely diverse patterns in us. Sometimes, in our most lucid moments, we seem to think clearly. When we have to make practical decisions, our thinking gets focused, and it directs our actions. But, during other times, there is no such clarity and focus.

Let's examine more closely our thoughts or whatever is an object of our attention. Once we stop long enough to see what is going on, we realize how fleeting our attention span really is. There are many kinds of thoughts, such as thoughts of family, of work, athletic events, or getting our children off to school. Our thoughts are not our brains and nervous systems. But rather, they are dependent on our brains, nervous systems, and bodily organs. In other words, our thoughts are a natural part of our created being. For example, our eyes make it possible for us to see where we are going, our ears to hear and our tongues to taste. All of this sensual input enters our brain and manifests itself in thought.

Again, all of our thoughts have a basis in our physical bodies, and some of our thoughts are determined by our physical condition. For example, if we have a headache, we move from other thoughts to the medicine cabinet. Hunger puts thoughts of food into our minds, so we head for the refrigerator. Disorders of body lead to disorders in thoughts. Mental derangements–in which people cannot distinguish between imagination and reality–arise in no small degree from physical derangements.

In prayer, we do not trample on the thought process, but we must learn to use it for God's purposes!

But it is self-evident that our normal thoughts are directly connected with our bodies. For example, we see other people and greet them. We hear their words and converse with them. We smell various odors, we touch knives and forks, and we taste foods. Our thoughts in daily life flow extensively from our senses. All of this is an inherent, God-ordained reality of human life on earth. Therefore, nothing that is said about prayer and our thoughts is an invitation or hint that we should stop using our organs of sense.

Our thoughts, like our dreams, often arise from half forgotten experiences that lie sleeping in our subconscious processes. What this tells us is that we should let our conscious moments feed our subconscious processes with good things. And this pattern can lead us to a creative prayer-life. In addition, we cannot help having all sorts of associations of ideas. One thought suggests another by a natural process. For many years, psychologists have been writing on the law of the association of ideas. Long before the psychologists, great novelists and dramatists have shown how the minds of human beings function by means of this law. And we would find it hard to make our way through any day of practical living without the power of our minds to make these connections. We see a neighbor, and various thoughts naturally arise in association with the one we see. Space relations, time relations, and interpersonal relations are all made possible by this law. Therefore, in prayer we do not trample upon this God-ordained mental process. Instead, we can use it!

Notably, not all thoughts are helpful to our prayers. In fact, there are certain types of thoughts which obstruct the way to a vital prayer-life. Consider three such types of thought: reverie, idle curiosity, and thoughts which arise from destructive emotions.

Reverie

Reverie is a free flow of thoughts which are largely disconnected from our real situation. For example, sometimes when we are listening to a lecture or a sermon, our minds drift off into far-away thoughts. Reverie is the opposite of concentration. It is distraction of mind. And often it is building castles in the air, or entertaining fanciful hopes. Frequently, our reveries revolve around our beloved egos. For our self-love is like the restless sea. Our thoughts return again and again to fanciful games of self-justification. Our reveries

94

may take us up to the high plateau of a fool's paradise or plunge us into the depths of a coward's hell.

In a memorable expression of honesty, the poet-clergyman John Donne tells of what may take place even in a saintly soul in prayer.

> **I throw myself down in my chamber and call in and invite God and His angels thither, and when they are there I neglect God and His angels for the noise of a fly, for the rattling of a coach, for the whining of a door. I talk on in the same posture of praying, eyes lifted up, knees bowed down, as though I prayed to God, and if God or His angels should ask me when I thought last of God in that prayer, I cannot tell. Sometimes I find that I had forgotten what I was about, but when I began to forget it I cannot tell. A memory of yesterday's pleasures, a fear of tomorrow's dangers, a straw under my knee, a noise in mine ear, a light in mine eye, an anything, a nothing, a fancy, a chimera in my brain troubles me in my prayer.**

Reverie is a universal problem in our prayer-life. In prayer we seek the *power from on high*, but in reverie there is no power. To be sure, there are times when we need to let our minds graze in the beautiful pastures of fantasy. But prayer is serious business. For we are in the presence of God, kneeling in awe and reverence, and opening our souls to God. In true prayer we experience godly sorrow for our sins, and we express our sincere desire to obey and serve God. We pray for the grace to be forgiven and the willingness to forgive any who misunderstand or mistreat us. We pray for the power to conquer temptation. And we yearn for the Holy Spirit to fill

95

our souls with the love of God and neighbor.

What is the answer to this universal tendency to be drawn away from God by our reveries? The answer takes us to a heart-principle of the devotional life. God spoke through the prophet Isaiah about this principle when he said:

> *Only in returning to me and waiting for me will you be saved. In quietness and confidence is your strength.*
> **Isaiah 30:15 NLT**

We cannot think of God all the time. When driving our cars, we have to look at the road, take in the traffic situation, observe the signs, know when to stop and go. When buying groceries, we have to observe the quality of the fruits and vegetables, and make judgments on what else to buy. So are our thoughts all along the way each day. Therefore, we must set aside times daily when we return to God and think solely of the things of God. This is the significance of regular times for public worship, Bible study and prayer.

It is this habit that gives meaning to Paul's call to pray without ceasing. For when we return to God at planned intervals, all else that we do is shaped by the mysterious sense of the presence of God.

The heart–principle of the devotional life: in returning to God is our strength.

Idle curiosity

Anything which tends to trivialize our relationships with others is an enemy of prayer in the biblical heritage. Idle curiosity usually concerns our thoughts about other people, and too often it sinks to the level of cheap gossip. We are all aware that there is a worthy place for human interest in one another. Our curiosity may arise from a sincere human interest which leads to giving the cup of cold water to the thirsty or housing to the homeless. And yet what threatens our prayers are the trains of thought disconnected from any desire to act in behalf of others. Sometimes these thoughts drift harmlessly into our minds and quickly pass away. Two people at a dinner table in a restaurant are whispering. What about? Another person is reading a letter intently. What is in it? Someone gets up in the middle of a sermon and walks out of the church. Why? Such idle curiosity is distracting, but, except for the waste of time and energy, it is relatively harmless.

Turn this around and look at the other side of it. Often idle curiosity, like a dreadful plague, leads us to say things about others which hurt or destroy them. The magazines devoted to gossip thrive on this universal idle curiosity. Their editors know where their market is, and they know that scandal and oddity need no supporting argument. Even in church circles, scandal may be played up again and again until we feel like crying out: Cease! Be done with lesser things! Press forward for the glory of God and the blessings for our fellow human beings!

One of the most notable differences between one human being and another can be seen in their powers of concentration. Some people make up their minds what they want to do, and they do it. They refuse to waste time and energy on day-dreams, distractions, and idle curiosity. Others live on the misty flats where their thoughts drift to and fro.

So, how do we stay focused in prayer and not allow the idle curiosity to take control? Here again we find the answer in the heart-principle of the devotional life: ***In returning shall be your strength.***

The two best ways of returning to God in prayer are by quoting familiar Bible verses and by praying simply and passionately that which we believe God to be and will do. In other words, we focus our attention back on God-who God is and what God has done.

Thoughts Arising from Destructive Emotions

At times, we all have feelings and attitudes that strike against our eternal happiness for ourselves or others. One of John Wesley's most interesting sermons, *Wandering Thoughts* distinguishes between those thoughts that are sinful and those that are not. He says:

> **Again: all thoughts which spring from sinful tempers are undoubtedly sinful. Such, for instance, are those that spring from a revengeful temper, from pride, or lust, or vanity. "An evil tree cannot bring forth good fruit," therefore if the tree be evil, so must the fruit be also.**

> **And so must those be which either produce or feed any sinful temper; those which either give rise to pride or vanity, to anger or love of the world, or confirm and increase these or any other unholy temper, passion, or affection. For not only whatever flows from evil is evil, but also whatever leads to it; whatever tends to alienate the soul from God, and to make or keep it "earthly, sensual, and devilish."**

All of us know what pride is: it is excessive self-love. It is thinking of ourselves more highly than we ought as is warned against here:

> *So I tell each of you not to think you are better than you really are.*
>
> **Romans 12:3 CEV**

Pride turns our thoughts away from God's purpose for us, makes us deaf even to constructive criticism, and leads us into a fatal complacency. Hatred leads to resentment, or sustained hostility which also in turn leads to vengeance. And all of these, whether taken in small doses or large, are poison to our prayer-life. Think of all the evil thoughts that arise from hatred! Because of these, Jesus emphasized his teaching on loving our enemies when he said:

> *But I tell you, love your enemies and pray for those who persecute you.*
>
> **Matthew 5:44 NIV**

And Paul, in imitating Jesus, says:

> *Do not take revenge, my friends, but leave room for God's wrath.*
>
> **Romans 12:19 NIV**

Lust produces thoughts of adultery, abnormal sexual practices, and betrayal. Greed leads to numberless evil thoughts and inhuman actions. Money is important, but, as the Bible teaches concerning the economic realm:

> *For the love of money is at the root of all kinds of evil.*
>
> **First Timothy 6:10 NLT**

And think of all the destructive thoughts awakened in our minds by despair when we are consumed with asking: Why me? What am I to do? What can I do? Why is everyone against me? Why doesn't anyone understand?

The risk of despairing or destructive thoughts is they may lead to a chronically negative attitude. However, at this point, a word of caution is also needed. Let us remember that we do not sin when evil thoughts merely flow into our consciousness. Jesus himself experienced clearly what Satan meant by his temptations. But those tempting thoughts did not lead him to sin. All kinds of thoughts may come and go without our yielding to them. We become sinners when we nurture evil thoughts and let them have room and board in the habitation of our souls.

How do we prevent distracting and negative thoughts from taking habitation in our souls? The best answer I know to all evil thoughts that arise from our destructive emotions is to pray earnestly for God, by grace, to cure and release us from those emotions. Those destructive thoughts are to be driven out by the power of God in Jesus Christ. This inner transformation has been called the expulsive power of a great affection or believing that God's grace in Christ is sufficient to cleanse us even of our destructive thoughts. This grace-filled cleansing is made possible through prayer, by which we become completely open to receive the love of Christ. The psalmist David was speaking of this cleansing love when he prayed to God:

> *Create in me a clean heart, O God, and put a new and right spirit within me.*
>
> **Psalm 51: 10 NRSV**

If this love of God in Christ is to be sustained against all the assaults of the enemy, we must follow the grand heart-principle of the devotional life: *In returning shall be your strength.* When our thoughts turn away from God, by God's grace we can return to him in focused prayer.

Questions for Reflection

1. What are the primary distractions or obstructing thoughts that most challenge your personal prayer-life?

2. Idle curiosity can be both distracting and destructive to our prayers. How can we make sure our "prayer chains" are free from this threat of idle curiosity and the sin of gossip?

3. Destructive emotions focus on the negative qualities of ourselves or others. Prayer requires focusing on the wonderful attributes of God. How would this shift of focus change our prayer for others–especially those with whom we are displeased?

person-to-Person connection

As we begin to pray without ceasing as Paul encourages, we must be prepared to respond readily to the regular distractions and negative obstructions to our prayers.

Memorize–or call to memory–a particular Bible verse that can serve to refocus your thoughts on the things of God such as Psalm 51:10 or Psalm 19:14.

Eight

Prayer and that One Defect

A combination of qualities is necessary to succeed in anything. In athletics, in addition to superior physical talents, a person needs determination, concentration, temperate habits, and the desire to win. In business, education, law, labor, farming, and daily work of any kind, many qualities are necessary for success.

Being a Christian also requires a combination of virtues such as faith, hope, love, and wisdom. But, by a strange twist, all we need is one major defect to put a blight upon our character and witness. That defect may put us under such a burden of guilt as to snuff out the inner witness. It may lead to doubts and fears which shut the door to faith. It will stand in the way of spiritual growth. And it often leads us into cheap excuses and tricky efforts to justify ourselves.

Moreover, any major defect will surely mar our Christian witness. Most basic of all is the inner damage done to our souls by a major defect. For, as Jesus said: *a house divided against itself cannot stand* (Mark 3:25). In the end such a defect is allowed to shut one out of the Kingdom of God.

There is a remarkable episode in Shakespeare's Hamlet in which Hamlet is looking down on a scene of drunkenness and revelry. He reflects on what he sees and observes that this is the problem of his people as a nation. The whole world judges

them by this folly or defect of behavior. Then he applies this
to the individual when he says:

> **So, oft it chances in particular men, That for some
> vicious mole of nature in them, As, in their birth–
> wherein they are not guilty, since nature cannot choose
> his origin.**

> **By the o'er growth of some complexion, oft breaking
> down the pales and forts of reason,or by some habit
> that too much o'er-leavens the form of plausive
> manners, that these men carrying, I say, the stamp of
> one defect being nature's livery, or fortune's star.**

> **Their virtues else–be they as pure as grace, As infinite
> as man may undergo shall in the general censure take
> corruption from that particular fault.**

We may read this as believers and say: "But surely a Christian
does not have any such major defect." And yet, we must all
recognize the plain fact of our imperfections. At the same
time, we must also hear the Master's call to move toward
perfection. Wesley preached on *Sin in Believers* where he
reminded his hearers that since ancient times Christians have
warned themselves of the continuing warfare between the
"flesh" and the "spirit." Even after we have been forgiven, we
are apt to falter and to fail the Savior who summons us to
righteousness. Paul also spoke of this struggle within believers
when he said:

> *The old sinful nature loves to do evil, which is just opposite
> from what the Holy Spirit wants. And the Spirit gives us
> desires that are opposite from what the sinful nature desires.*

> *The two forces are constantly fighting each other, and your choices are never free from this conflict.*
>
> **Galatians 5:17 NLT**

Wesley pointed out that even though we are *new creations* we still may not have *the whole mind which was in Christ*.

What defect so mars our lives as Christians as to reduce our effectiveness and witness? For one person it will be one thing and for another something else. It might be anger which hardens into bitterness. It might be some habit, like alcoholism or drug addiction, which maintains a demonic grip on a person who is struggling to grow in Christ. Or it might be needless ignorance. We are all ignorant, but there is such a thing as unnecessary ignorance when we refuse to know or understand something for fear that the understanding may change us. It may be that our defect is that we are too easily hurt.

That one defect may be an uncontrolled tongue which spews out venom in anger or assassinates a character in gossip. Or it might be an easy-going sleep-walking contentment with mediocrity. Mediocrity is the measure of nothing. There is an authority about the best. That's why there is a glory about anyone who opens his or her soul to Christ. For it is in that act we line ourselves up with the best who has ever walked on this earth.

Once more, that one defect may be that we believe in Christ but do not believe in the church. This is an error both of the head and the heart. For there never has been, is not now, and cannot ever be any sustained expression of God's good news in Christ apart from a community of believers. Without

a community of faith, Christian experience and witness
are reduced to fitful occasions of enthusiasm and fleeting
moments of history. Isolated Christians do not last long, and
they are apt to have little or no influence in the world. For
this reason, in the Old Testament, God worked through the
people of Israel. And, in the New Testament, while there is
always the Master's concern for each person, there is also
his concern to form the disciples into a body of believers.
In addition, we can never forget that he came preaching the
gospel of the Kingdom of God which inherently is communal.
We must all come to grips with what our own major defect is.
It may be something other than anything mentioned in the
foregoing paragraphs. But whatever that one defect may be,
there is the promise of victory over it by the grace of God.

God's grace is sufficient for us in all circumstances, and all defects.

Overcoming the Defect

Many people think that the best answer is to be found in
resolutions. We resolve to overcome that one defect. But
the Bible does not give much basis for hope in our human
resolutions. To be sure, it may be helpful to make a resolution
to indicate our determination to gain the mastery of a defect,
but much more is needed. So in the Bible we hear God's call
to reach beyond our human efforts and to enter into the realm
of earnest prayer.
What we require, in order to come to grips with some really
basic defect, is first, the help we can get from God, as well

as the help from ourselves and others. Many times we feel as though we are going down for the third time, and our yearning for victory is often desperate. God, in his infinite love and wisdom, has provided the way to victory over that one defect, namely, through earnest sustained prayer. And when this passionate personal prayer is combined with the intercessory prayers and supportive fellowship within the community of faith, there are vast resources available from God for giving us the help we need to overcome and conquer.

Victory through Prayer

When we pray for God to help us, we need to be specific. We need to focus on that one defect, known to us, to those who love us most, and to God, and to pray for divine help for victory over it just for today. And when we do, in full earnestness and faith, God will give us the victory. Paul reminds us that God's grace is sufficient for us in all circumstances when he told the church in Corinth what Jesus had said to him:

> *Each time he said to me, "My gracious favor is all you need. My power moves best in your weakness."*
> **Second Corinthians 12:9 NLT**

In witness to the fulfillment of this promise, numberless Christians throughout the centuries have told the great story of how God has given them the victory through Jesus Christ.

Paul, of course, is our master spokesman on the life-changing power of God through Jesus Christ. In one of his finest moments of inspiration, he says:

> *I see in my members another law at war with the law of my mind and making me captive to the law of sin which dwells*

106

in my members. Wretched man that I am! Who will deliver me from this body of death? Thanks be to God through Jesus Christ our Lord!"

Romans 7:23-25

Then Paul continues:

There is therefore now no condemnation for those who are in Christ Jesus. For the law of the Spirit of life in Christ Jesus has set me free from the law of sin and death

Romans 8:1-2 NRSV

And another inspired writer confirms all this with this statement:

For whatever is born of God conquers the world; and this is the victory that conquers the world, our faith

First John 5:4 NRSV

Above all, we need to understand that every major defect is against God and others and ourselves. Therefore, beyond any particular defect, we need to pray for such a flood tide of love for God, for others, and for ourselves that any soul-threatening, life-destroying defect will be overcome by divine grace. Here our prayers will be focused on our attaining that inward holiness which leads to outward holiness. This inward holiness is the demonstration of loving God with all our heart, soul, mind, and strength, and loving our neighbor as ourselves. This kind of love comes only by grace through faith. It is of utmost importance to believe, in the name of Jesus, that this prayer will be answered

You haven't done this before. Ask, using my name, and you will receive, and you will have abundant joy.

John 16:24 NLT

Christian history, since the days of the apostles, bears witness to this empowering grace of Jesus Christ that has overcome soul-threatening defects in believers in all ages and all walks of life. For Christ came to set us free from what holds us in bondage. There is no such defect in our character from which we cannot be delivered with the help of Almighty God. However, victory requires that we do our part. We must realize with godly sorrow the seriousness of whatever drags us down and separates us from God. And we must pray with confidence and strive passionately and persistently for God's deliverance believing it will happen. Then the promised help is on its way to make us more than conquerors through Jesus Christ our Lord.

Questions for Reflection

1. Each of us has something about us that can become a blight on our character or witness. What "major defect" may be getting in the way of your fuller relationship with God or others?

2. Our one major defect at times keeps us from praying for others for fear that we are not "worthy" to come before God. When have you avoided praying for someone because your "defect" made you feel unworthy to ask?

3. Victory over our defect also comes by allowing others within the community of faith to intercede, or pray on our behalf for our release from the defect. Who are individuals in your community of faith who you trust to help release you?

person-to-Person Connection

Identify your "major defect" that may be preventing a fuller and more intimate life with God and others.

Begin praying daily, as Paul did, that God will release you from this defect and that God will use this "weakness" to make you strong. Identify trusted friends in the faith to partner with you to pray for your release from this defect.

Nine

Prayer and Our Fears

Everyone knows what fear is. It is a basic uneasiness about the past, present, or future. It is that "common quaking in the breast" which we all feel when we have lost something or are about to lose something that is precious to us: a dear one, life, health, reputation, property, liberty. More often than not, our fears focus on the future when we ask the questions: What is going to happen to us? Where are we to go?

There are fears that are rooted in reality, but many of them are imaginary. They have little or no basis in the real world. We see a small cloud and imagine a storm. We see a drop of blood and suspect a murder. We expect the worst and dread it. We take a little balloon shaped like a lion and blow it up into a monster.

One of the most primal emotions in all creatures, including humans, is fear. But the fear which often grips us the most is fear of the unknown. And, unfortunately, unless we fix our gaze on something other than the vast darkness of the unknown, we tend to become paralyzed in our faith.

Where our fears are concerned our imagination plays havoc with us. Today we are constantly led to exaggerate the dangers because of the numberless news reports on threatening events. Murder, robbery, drug addiction, alcoholism, rape, and even wrong living unpunished by the law alarm us.

Nuclear destruction, pollution, overpopulation, starvation, and terrorism stalk about before us like giants. *Fear hath more devils than vast hell can hold.* But whether imagined or real, fear incapacitates us for effective living.

Every Christian knows this destructive power of fear and, with God's help, can find a creative response to it. Every Christian who practices the life of prayer can and will discover how best to handle fear. Through prayer, our gaze is shifted from looming–even unknown–threats to the known promises of God.

Through prayer, we shift our gaze from looming threats to the promises of God.

Through prayer, we become calm. Anxiety gradually slips away, and simple faith emerges. We begin to think about things as they are, and our imagination gives way to sober thought. We take our eyes off ourselves and turn them toward God. Moreover, in prayer we think of Jesus and his courage in facing the most awesome opposition and suffering, and our fears often pale in comparison. Courage breeds courage, and when we focus on the courage of Christ in prayer, we, too, find the courage to respond.

In his own journey through much darkness, our Savior embodied the ability to move forward in faith. And he taught and expected his followers to do likewise. In fact, Jesus prepared them to face many circumstances that would undoubtedly evoke fear. But his words of calm assurance called them to focus forward instead of faltering in fear.

> *Peace I leave with you; my peace I give to you. I do not give to you as the world gives. Do not let your hearts be troubled, and do not let them be afraid.*
>
> **John 14:27 NRSV**

On the verge of his own suffering and death, and in anticipation of their own, Jesus reminded them of a future filled with promise and hope greater and larger than any fear.

In prayer, the Christian can also call to mind some of the great verses of the Bible emerging from the never-ending encounters with fear. These verses spoke to the needs of those who went before us, and they still speak to our needs and fears today. In addition, we can receive renewed courage by reading or singing some of the great hymns of the Church through which we find wonderful mysterious spiritual resources for conquering fear in the fellowship of believers.

> *O God, our help in ages past,*
> *our hope for years to come,*
> *our shelter from the stormy blast,*
> *and our eternal home!*
>
> *O God Our Help in Ages Past*
> Isaac Watts, 1719

> *When I tread the verge of Jordan,*
> *bid my anxious fear subside;*
> *death of death and hell's destruction,*
> *land me safe on Canaan's side.*
> *Song of praises, song of praises,*
> *I will ever give to thee;*
> *I will ever give to thee.*
>
> *Guide Me, O Thou Great Jehovah*
> William Williams, 1745

Be still, my soul: the Lord is on your side
Bear patiently the cross of grief or pain;
Leave to your God to order and provide;
in every change God faithful will remain.
Be still, my soul: your best, your heavenly friend
through thorny ways leads to a joyful end.

Be Still, My Soul
Katherin von Schlegel, 1752

We turn now to the most important reason why prayer conquers fear. When we pray, we are looking to the One who alone is greater than the sum total of all our fears. The only final answer to fear must be found in resources that are more powerful than fear. These flow into our souls from God through faith, and faith means putting our trust in God no matter what happens. The great characters of the Bible conquered fear by turning from themselves to God. They found the answer in God, before whom all our fears are defeated. For God graciously acts to free us from our bondage to fears. The psalmist said, *I will fear no evil.* Why? Because he could say also: *For thou art with me.* Isaiah experienced this great resource when God said to him:

> **Do not fear, for I am with you, do not be afraid, for I am**
> **your God; I will strengthen you, I will help you, I will**
> **uphold you with my victorious right hand.**
>
> **Isaiah 41:10 NRSV**

When we experience the presence of the living Christ, we know and believe these words of a great hymn:

> **Jesus! The name that charms our fears,**
> **that bids our sorrows cease;**
> **'tis music in the sinner's ears,**

'tis life, and health, and peace.

O For A Thousand Tongues to Sing
Charles Wesley, 1734

Paul, in Romans 8:35-37, not only asked, *Who shall separate us from the love of Christ?* He specified the enemies which threaten us: *Shall tribulation, or distress, or persecution, or famine, or nakedness, or peril, or sword?* Then he who had experienced these evils added, *No, in all these things we are more than conquerors through him who loved us.*

Further still, when we pray we are prepared for daily living, and we find our souls purified. For instance, we may engage in dishonesty in dealing with others, and no matter how subtle this dishonesty can become, it is a major source of fear. Tell a lie and you have to remember what you said. Dishonesty in interpersonal relations breeds lies upon lies and consequently fears upon fears.

The wicked flee when no one pursues, but the righteous are bold as a lion.

Proverbs 28:1 NRSV

Prayer cleanses the soul and sets it free from those subtle forms of deception which are fertile ground for fear. For this reason, prayer conquers fear through love. Unholiness breeds fear, but love conquers fear. And in prayer, we open our souls toward the love of Christ just as the flowers open themselves toward the sun. As a result, in the processes of daily living in prayer, we experience the victory over fear.

There is no fear in love, but perfect love casts out fear

First John 4:18 NRSV

In our love for God and neighbor, we experience the confidence that comes from basic honesty. And love coupled with faith is the best possible equipment for going into the future with God. Jesus said:

> *Fear not, little flock, for it is your Father's good pleasure to give you the kingdom*
>
> **Luke 12:32 RSV**

In that realm we gain the mastery over fear by the grace of God and believing that God desires only the best for us.

So, not by accident or coincidence, but through prayer and faith, we gain peace and bear witness to the powerful presence of God's abiding love in our lives. And we are even more assured that God does and will continue to give victory over fear as we stand in witness of the long procession of the faithful who, by prayer and faith, overcame martyrdom, torture and persecution.

Questions for Reflection

1. What fears do you find are most distracting or even paralyzing for you?

2. Fears, especially of the unknown, almost always loom larger than reality. What fear do you have (or have you had) that seems to loom larger causing doubt in God?

3. Again, central to prayer is refocusing more on God and less on a situation. From that perspective, how might your fears be minimized through Christ-centered prayer?

person-to-Person Connection

In the face of fear, we often need something to draw our attention back to Christ so we focus less on the looming threat. Develop the discipline of singing regularly a hymn or song of praise that proclaims the power of Christ to conquer all. When fears or threats come to mind, refocus your heart and mind by singing this song.

> *I will call upon the Lord,*
> *who is worthy to be praised.*
> *So shall I be saved from my enemies.*
> *I will call upon the Lord.*

> *The Lord liveth, and blessed be the Rock;*
> *And let the God of my salvation be exalted!*
> *The Lord liveth, and blessed be the Rock;*
> *And let the God of my salvation be exalted!*

Michael O'Shields

Ten

Prayer and Loneliness

Loneliness is universal. Everybody knows what it is. We may be seated in a room full of people and still feel lonely. We may be walking in a shopping center crowded with people and be overwhelmed with loneliness. We may have a husband or wife, children and grandchildren, friends and neighbors-each of whom we love-and still feel lonely. To be sure, this is not the same as the loneliness which comes when we have no one who is really close to us. But whether we have close family and friends or not, there is a mysterious sense of loneliness that haunts the human spirit. Each of us is a solitary soul. In a true sense, each of us is an island. Matthew Arnold, in his poem, *To Marguerite,* gives voice to this human emotion.

> **Yes! In the sea of life enisl'd,**
> **With echoing straits between us thrown,**
> **Dotting the shoreless watery wild,**
> **We mortal millions live alone.**

What is this loneliness of which the poets have spoken and of which I speak here? What is this solitariness that even the dearest lovers feel? And what is it that even our closest friends experience? It could be called the longing for God. Alfred North Whitehead said: *Religion is what the individual does with his own solitariness.*

Of course, the whole of religion is not a mere response to loneliness, but it is certainly a part of it. Our solitariness does not drive us to God simply because we are left out of a social group or a circle of intimate friends. Yet, there is the unalterable fact that each of us is walled into a private world. You are not I; I am not you.

We are born one by one and die one by one. Each of us has his or her own experiences. Our feelings are private. Our decisions, however influenced by circumstances or other people, are made by our own individual wills. When we tie this fact of our solitariness to the fact of our finitude, we begin to get an overwhelming message of loneliness. Here let us change the image from an island to a piece of cork bobbing up and down on an alien sea. No matter how many other corks there are, the undeniable sense of our isolation is there. And this image suggests both our isolation and our flimsiness.

We may pause here to note that this isolation has nothing to do with whether we are male or female, black or white, yellow or red, ignorant or learned, rich or poor. It probes beneath the skin and goes beyond all cultural barriers. In fact, all those distinctions become relatively trivial and even comical when we consider this universal fact of solitariness. No man or woman on earth can ever escape the unalterable reality of this fundamental isolation.

We all have a very basic need to be known and to know others.

Few things are more painful and destructive for human beings than the man-made injustices which feed off of exclusiveness. Another way to think of this is to imagine being thrown into an alien cosmic realm, alone, isolated, solitary. Here, even though we are all alike, we may still experience the sense of being lost in an apparently indifferent cosmos. I know of few thoughts more tragic than that of being an unknown entity in an unknowing Universe. We all have a very basic need to be known and to know others.

What has all this to do with prayer? Everything. For loneliness, in its deeper dimensions, is the longing for God. It may even be one of the primary means by which the Holy Spirit summons us to open our souls to the living Word of God. People often ask, "Where is God? Why doesn't God tell me what I most need to know?" The answer is that God does speak to each one of us. But we are deaf and do not hear, stubborn and will not understand. And yet when we enter into a devoted prayer-life, we create the time and space to experience, to hear, and to know that God is with us.

God's Invitation

God is with us in our loneliness and solitariness drawing us toward the life-giving, faith-relationship with God. It is as though God were saying to each of us, "Are you lonely, isolated? Then turn to your Maker in whom there can be enduring meaning." If we feel like a piece of cork tossed about on a stormy sea, then the Spirit of the living God is speaking to us, saying, "Come, son or daughter, behold my love for you in Jesus Christ, and put your trust in the One who is the Master of the storm-tossed sea."

In this mood, as we pray, the presence of the Holy Spirit is felt again, and we know that we are not alone. For God is with us. In short, the mysterious sense of loneliness is God's call to commune with our Maker, and to receive the divine blessings.

As we pray in our loneliness, it is particularly important to have in mind certain great passages of the Bible. Not just any passages will do. For we require, in this deep mysterious experience of isolation, those passages in which the inspired writers felt what we feel. They, too, were profoundly lonely.

> *Out of the depths I cry to thee, O Lord!*
>
> **Psalm 130:1 NRSV**

> *My God, my God! Why have you forsaken me? Why do you remain so distant. Why do you ignore my cries for help? Every day I call to you, but you do not answer. Every night you hear my voice, but I find no relief.*
>
> **Psalm 22:1-2 NLT**

Within the biblical heritage, we also hear the cries of loneliness from God's faithful servants who experienced isolation even in the midst of, and sometimes as a result of, their obedience to God.

> *Elijah was afraid and fled for his life. He went to Beersheba, a town in Judah, and he left his servant there. Then he went on alone into the desert, traveling all day. He sat down under a solitary broom tree and prayed that he might die. "I have had enough, Lord," he said. "Take my life, for I am no better than my ancestor...."*
>
> *But the Lord said to him, "What are you doing here, Elijah?"*
>
> *Elijah replied, "I have zealously served the Lord God Almighty. But the people of Israel have broken their covenant with you, torn down your altars, and killed every one of your prophets. I alone am left, and now they are trying to kill me, too."*
>
> **First Kings 19:3-4 & 9-10 NLT**

And yet, in prayer, as those servants cried out to God, God met them where they were—in the midst of their despair—reminding them of God's mighty and steadfast presence, even in a gentle whisper. They were powerfully reminded: We are not alone.

The words of Jesus come home to us in these times of our loneliness:

> *Come to me, all you who are weary and burdened, and I will give you rest.*
>
> Matthew 11:28 NIV

> *And remember, I am with you always.*
>
> Matthew 28:20 NRSV

Here, too, we find the meaning of many of the hymns which have stood the test of time. For their writers were keenly sensitive to this pervasive human condition of solitariness with its consequent sense of loneliness.

> *A mighty fortress is our God,*
> *A bulwark never failing;*
> *Our helper he amid the flood*
> *Of mortal ills prevailing...*
>
> *A Mighty Fortress is Our God*
> Martin Luther, 1529

> *When other helpers fail and comforts flee,*
> *Help of the helpless, O abide with me.*
>
> *Abide With Me*
> Henry Lyte, 1847

Somewhere in the midst of our loneliness we discover why private prayer is enriched abundantly by public worship. For the Holy Spirit works through the support we receive in the community of prayer and faith to bring back to life and memory the reality that we are part of a community of faith. We are not alone. Then, in private prayer, the soul, as if it were nurtured and fed by the rich input of hymns, liturgy, sacraments, prayers, Scripture, preaching, and sharing, is prepared for God. In all of these, God's grace acts mysteriously to give us a more vital prayer-life. And our solitary souls thus open themselves to the enduring, joy-creating fellowship with God through Jesus Christ.

Herein also lies the reason why we cannot help but love God. In the midst of our isolation and loneliness, through prayer, God breaks in to remind us who God is and how much God cares for us. Most of the time we human beings never see God. Instead, we see the world around us. We see other people; and in part know who they are. But we can't see God, and we do not realize who God really is. We have eyes but do not see. Then, in certain holy moments, the veil is removed, and we get a vision of God. And in this vision, we behold God as perfect love. We know God to be the One who created us out of that unlimited love for us. We know God as the Fountain of all possibilities of grace in Jesus Christ. And when this revelation comes, we cannot help but love God.

When we see a rose, we delight in it. When we see the mountains in their fall glory, spread out before us like a magnificent garden of colors, we feel their splendor. When we see the starry heavens, we stand in awe. And when we lift up our heads and are given the eyes of faith to behold the glory of God, we cannot help but love and adore God. And in response, we cannot help but serve God.

Sometimes such a vision may come to us in the solitariness of our private devotions; sometimes, in the fellowship with other believers; sometimes, during public worship when we hear the Word, sing the hymns, and feel the power of each other's prayers. But for all who truly seek him, God graciously grants the assurance of the divine presence. And we then know: We are not alone.

Questions for Reflection

1. Loneliness is a universal experience. At some point, we all feel lonely. When did your own loneliness lead to isolation when you could not speak to others? When did it result in an ability to speak with or pray to God?

2. When has your obedience in faith led to feelings of loneliness or isolation?

3. When and how have you been re-connected with God and others in prayer and public worship?

person-to-Person Connection

The means of grace, including prayer, reading Scripture, public worship, and communion, are ways in which we encounter and experience the presence and love of God. The means of grace are also essential to overcoming feelings of loneliness and isolation.

The next time you experience feelings of isolation and loneliness, open yourself to God's presence and the presence of the community of faith through Bible study, prayer, public worship, and communion.

When you are engaged in Bible study and worship in the community of faith, also take note of others who seem isolated or lonely and extend the grace and presence of Jesus Christ to them.

Eleven

Prayer and Temptation

Temptation is fascination with anything that is destructive. A desire for anything good, however, is not usually considered temptation. We do not think of the desire for truth, or goodness, or beauty as temptation. Nor do we think that when a person wants a good job, he or she is being tempted. Temptation is desire, but, it is desire for the wrong thing, for anything that can potentially harm ourselves or others. In Milton's *Paradise Lost*, when Eve took the fruit, she was convinced that she was choosing good. But as we know, that choice is known as the beginning of all human temptation.

On the face of it, it would seem that people would not want anything which is harmful or destructive, but this is not the case. We human beings are so made that we tend to see only the delights of a particular act and lose sight of the damaging consequences. We can easily talk ourselves into supposing that there will be no such consequences. And sometimes, even when we know we will be bringing harm to ourselves and to those we love, we go ahead in our folly. Often we live in a fool's paradise and become victims of the tyranny of the immediate present. This is why I speak of temptation as the fascination with the destructive–which is often, at the moment, not seen as destructive.

Human nature is a curious thing. It has an inexhaustible capacity to be fascinated or bewitched by that which strikes against it. Sigmund Freud often spoke about a "death instinct" or a kind of death-wish. Unfortunately, this is often more real than we might like to believe. For example, think of all the people who work incessantly for what leads to their own unhappiness!

In light of this attraction to what destroys us, the biblical writers also recognized the importance of coming to grips with temptation. The work of Moses and the prophets was in no small degree concerned with the never-ending problem of Israel's temptation to turn away from the Lord God by lapsing into idolatry and immorality. Jesus warned against yielding to temptation. And Jesus also warned about those who quickly respond to the Word of God but who, having no root, *in time of temptation fall away* (Luke 8:13).

The Master also spoke of temptation in the great prayer he left with his disciples. No one seems to know quite how to interpret the words: *And lead us not into temptation.* For it's hard to imagine how God would actually lead his children into temptation. Here we need to remember the words from the Epistle of James:

> *No one, when tempted, should say, "I am being tempted by God"; for God cannot be tempted by evil and he himself tempts no one. But one is tempted by one's own desire, being lured and enticed by it.*
>
> **James 1:13-14 NRSV**

Whatever else Jesus meant in the Lord's Prayer, we must also note that he moved immediately from the words about temptation to those about deliverance: *But deliver us from evil.* In the Lord's Prayer, then, we find the longing for victory over temptation expressed in the powerful petition for deliverance from evil.

Prayers to Overcome

In the biblical context, there are two reasons why we should pray to overcome temptation. The first is to avoid the harmful consequences of evil deeds. The second is to grow spiritually through the experience of gaining the victory over temptation. Let us consider these briefly.

Prayers to Avoid Consequences

Our heavenly Father calls us to prayer before the times of temptation so that we may avoid the destructive consequences of wrongdoing. Jesus said to his drowsy disciples: *Why do you sleep? Rise and pray that you may not enter into temptation* (Luke 22:46). Here, Jesus suggests that our prayers prepare us in advance so that no strong temptation will have sway over us. This is undoubtedly one of the soundest principles of the spiritual life. If we wait to pray when the temptations come, we are almost sure to fail. To knowingly face temptation without first being clothed in prayer is comparable to engaging in battle without suiting up with armor. If we follow Jesus by girding ourselves in advance through prayer, then we can gain the victory over temptation with God's help.

Prayers to Grow Strong

Paul also speaks about the effect of temptation on us when he said:

> *If you think you are standing strong, be careful, for you, too, may fall into the same sin. But remember, that the temptations that come into your life are no different from what others experience. And God is faithful. He will keep the temptation from becoming so strong that you can't stand*

up against it. When tempted, he will show you a way out so that you will not give in to it.

First Corinthians 10:12-13 NLT

Paul's words have as much relevance today as they did for the Christians at Corinth. These verses indicate that we become strong through encounters with temptation when we rely on the grace and presence of God. We, as Christians, are to live our new life in Christ in the midst of the world where we are constantly faced with temptations. This does not mean that we are to engage in a weak and sentimental flirting with temptation. Rather, it means that in our daily lives, temptation is inevitable. And when rooted in Christ, we grow spiritually through our encounters with it. It is no sin to be tempted. Jesus, himself was tempted in Matthew 4:1-11. He was *in every respect. . . Tempted as we are, yet without sin* (Hebrews 4:15). Our sin comes not from the temptation, but rather from not being prepared in advance to rise above temptation.

Temptation is more than being allured by the destructive. It is an opportunity for victory!

In this context, temptation is more than being allured by the destructive; it is also an opportunity for victory. Temptation is God's way of testing us and seeing what we are made of. So temptation confronts us with a danger to be avoided and, at the same time, a challenge to be faced. In the Epistle of James, we read about this simultaneous temptation and potential victory when he says:

My brothers and sisters, whenever you face trials of any kind, consider it nothing but joy, because you know that the testing of your faith produces endurance; and let endurance have its full effect, so that you may be mature and complete, lacking in nothing.

James 1:2-4 NRSV

Here again, it is assumed that those who meet these trials and temptations successfully will do so with God's help. And God readily helps us in temptation through prayer.

The need for prayer is all the more evident when we note that our moods also effect how we respond to temptation. For example, when we have been terribly disappointed, and our world has collapsed around us, we are apt to sink like stones in the face of temptations of one sort or another. Sustained anxiety also tends to set us up for defeat. Kierkegaard went so far as to say that anxiety is the primal source of sin. Grief and tragedy often make us vulnerable. At other times poor health or other life challenges cause us to lose morale before the challenges of life. And as a result, we falter and fall into temptation and sin.

Through prayer, the power of God is made perfect in our weakness.

Morale is the will to enter each day with hope and promise. But there are many times and circumstances when we are so overwhelmed by events, so shattered by grief, and so confused by anxiety that we are temptation-prone. In such times and

129

moods, we need especially to pray for God's help so that we may be more than conquerors through faith in Christ. The power of God *is made perfect in weakness* (Second Corinthians 12:9). However, we can only obtain moral and spiritual strength when we realize and acknowledge we need God's help.

In and through all our temptations, we must look to Jesus Christ because he is the only source and *perfecter of our faith* (Hebrews 12:2). We must look to Jesus because he is the conqueror of the severest temptations. And through him, we can draw near to the throne of grace with confidence *that we may receive mercy and find grace to help in time of need* (Hebrews 4:16). In this connection, the word "grace" is one of the most beautiful words in the New Testament which Paul, more than any other, put into our Christian vocabulary. What does it mean? "Grace" means God's immediate presence and power at work in us through Jesus Christ. God's grace is the divine love and power flowing into and through our souls. As a result of God's grace, God graciously pardons our sins. God's act of pardoning us through the merits of Jesus Christ is God's act for us. God's presence as the pardoning God is in us and is experienced and witnessed by us. Likewise, in times of temptation, when we experience our frailty and hold fast to Christ, we can experience the in flowing grace of God. As a result, we are given the power to look temptation in the face and to drive it away.

God's grace which is in us is much greater than the evil forces in the world around us. As the inspired writer put it: *Greater is he that is in you, than he that is in the world* (First John 4:4 KJV).

Questions for Reflection

1. Temptation, like loneliness, is universal for all humans. When has God delivered you from temptation so you were able to avoid the consequences which could have followed?

2. When has your mood or circumstances made you more susceptible to temptation?

3. When have you prayed prayers of protection for others so they would be guarded from temptation?

person-to-Person Connection

The promise and reality of God's presence in prayer reminds us that God is stronger than any and all temptations.

Before entering a situation in which you know you may be tempted, call on God's promise as found in the Bible by praying repeatedly:

Greater is God that is in me, than is this temptation in the world.

Twelve

Prayer and Suffering

There are times when prayer is the only thing that can keep us going. It has been observed that the ancient Greeks, in their religion, assumed that people were never sick or sorry. However, the sense of tragedy moves through the Judeo-Christian heritage like a mighty theme. The episodes of biblical history are perpetual reminders that sorrow, suffering, pain, spiritual disaster, and death are substantive factors in the history of Israel as well as in the lives of the apostles and other Christians. Rachel weeping for her children and the prophets suffering for their convictions tell the story.

Jesus came on the scene not as a happy warrior, but as the Suffering Servant.

> *He was despised and rejected by others; a man of suffering and acquainted with infirmity.*
>
> **Isaiah 53:3 NRSV**

God does not promise us that, when we put our trust in God, everything will work out all right on earth. Neither the prophets nor Jesus had an easy time of it. And the apostles encountered sorrow, suffering, and martyrdom.

Why do people suffer? Or, why do the innocent suffer? There is no adequate answer to those questions. Sometimes we suffer because of our sins and mistakes, sometimes because of the sin and folly of others. But often we suffer without any justifiable reason. All we can say is that we know God is good, we know God loves us and suffers with us, and gives us the strength we need in the midst of our suffering and grief.

The Certainty of Suffering

When we look at life itself, we realize how often tragedy overtakes us. We can easily understand what an anonymous actor felt when he said, "The theater of all my acts has fallen." If we are spared for a time, we still know that suffering is sure to come, for death is inevitable including the loss of those with whom our lives have been woven together in love and friendship for many years. Memories of those precious ones may linger, but they are as mere shadows compared to the touch of a hand, the sound of a voice, the warmth of a presence.

God makes provision for our suffering and grief through prayer.

How can the shattered relationships be mended when death has had its say? Can we pick up the fragments of our broken dreams and start over? Can the love and friendship of a lifetime be begun again when the evening is drawing near? No. What then? Has the God who made us forsaken us? Has the Christ who redeemed us cast us off? Has the Holy Spirit who comforted us abandoned us? God forbid. What then? Our Loving God, in infinite love and wisdom, has made provision for us in the hours of our suffering and grief. God summons us to enter into an ever-renewing faith. God calls us to prayer. And when, amid our suffering and grief, we open our souls to the Holy Spirit in prayer, we receive at least four blessings of supreme importance.

Provision of Presence

The first is that, despite our sorrow and grief, we become more profoundly aware of the presence of God. In the depths of our weakness and inadequacy, God has given us the vision of the glory and the warmth of the divine presence. We know, as millions before us have known, that the Father will never leave us or forsake us. For God made us, and we are the sheep of God's pasture as Psalm 100:3 tells us. Therefore, through suffering and grief, God works to perfect us and to make us aware of God's presence.

Provision of God's Glory

Closely related to this is a second blessing from our prayer-life that God brings through suffering and grief, namely, a more profound awareness of the height and depth and riches of God's glory and grace. It is one thing to know that God goes with us through life and tragedy and death. It is another thing to become increasingly aware of the vast ranges of God's mysterious love in redeeming, nurturing, and empowering us for mission. Paul, who knew suffering, caught something of the spirit of this when he cried:

> *O the depth of the riches and wisdom and knowledge of God! How unsearchable are his judgments and how inscrutable his ways! For who has known the mind of the Lord? Or who has been his counselor? Or who has given a gift to him, to receive a gift in return? For from him and through him and to him are all things. To him be the glory forever. Amen.*
> **Romans 11:33-36 NRSV**

Out of the depths of suffering and grief comes the vision of the greatness and glory of God. And by grace we are enabled to sing again.

Provision of the Fellowship of Believers

In times of suffering a third special blessing comes to us, namely, through the prayers and presence of others we receive a new appreciation of the care and support which comes from the fellowship of believers. In the church we find that others are caring for us and suffering with us. And the Holy Spirit mysteriously uses their comforting hands and prayers to give us the grace to see life through. Then, as we pray during the lonely hours of the night, we thank God for the ties that bind our hearts in Christian love and for the sympathizing tear.

> **Through our suffering, we are placed in a special position to help others.**

Provision of New Avenues to Serve

A fourth blessing of prayer in the times of suffering is the new vision of service. When we have lost all–or what seems like all–the Holy Spirit graciously opens up avenues of service on which we can move into the future. God makes us aware that as long as we are on earth, as long as we are called upon to live and breathe, we are summoned by God to do what we can to help others.

All who have known grief are placed in a special position to help others who grieve. All who have suffered greatly may feel more deeply than others the hurt of human beings and enter upon the life of service with a greater capacity for sympathy and for thoughtful deeds. When we suffer real tragedy, we receive new priorities, new values, new ways of understanding the difference between what is important and what is trivial. This too, by God's grace, gives us the power to serve more productively and creatively in God's holy mission.

In short, we behold anew the glory of God in Jesus Christ who came not to be ministered to but to serve. Then, by the grace of God, we strive to walk as Jesus walked. And when our life on earth is done, we know that we shall have an opportunity for an everlasting adventure with God and with all who love God in the life after death. We can live with the hope of being reunited with those we love. For we know that God is not encouraging us to form beautiful friendships on earth only to see them destroyed by death. Instead, God employs even our suffering to make a way for God's grace so that in life–and in death–God's glory is manifested.

Questions for Reflection

1. Suffering, like temptation and loneliness, is again known to us all. How is suffering foundational to our faith unlike other religions who deny that the faithful should suffer?

2. How and when have you experienced God's presence in the midst of suffering?

3. God gives us the gift of the fellowship of believers to comfort us and care for us in our suffering. How is it challenging for you to share your suffering with other believers?

4. How and when has your own suffering opened up avenues for you to serve others as an instrument of God's grace?

person-to-Person Connection

God promised to transform our suffering and loss into new opportunities for us to serve others in Jesus' name.

Think about a recent loss or difficulty you have suffered. Pray that God will use this situation to open up new avenues of service through you.

Thirteen

Prayer for Healing and Intercession

When we pray for the sick and for others in need, we are engaging in intercessory prayer. At its best, this high level of prayer is expressing to God our deep concern for others. In intercessory prayer, in the light of the biblical revelation, we are aware that God's love and energies go beyond natural laws and processes. The God who created the universe-and whose energies pervade it–transcends it. In intercessory prayer, our spirits are opened to the vast resources of God other than those of nature. Such prayer leads us directly into the realm of God's redeeming and healing grace.

Believe It or Not

Many people today, however, find it hard to believe in intercessory prayer. But why? For one thing, they are convinced that we live in a universe where events occur only according to law. In other words, they believe humans are what they are, and their consequences will be what they will be. Accordingly, people are what they are largely because of the laws of sowing and reaping. If this is the case, then why should we pray for the sick and for others in misery? In this way of thinking, then God cannot act except through the laws of nature. But this clearly limits God's sovereign ability to not only create–but to impact the physical universe.

There are various realms of reality: only one of which is

physical. In addition to the physical, there is the realm of the human mind which has its affects upon our bodies. Also, there is the realm of God's grace which also affects both mind and body. There is much in all realms of Being of which we know very little. What we do believe is that the Sovereign God created all these realms, the physical, the body, the mind, all through grace. So we go ahead with our intercessory prayers and leave the results to God. For praying for each other lifts up all these realms and trusts God to work in all.

We wonder: Isn't God too great to deal in the small details of our lives?

Nothing Too Big—or Too Small

Some people today find it hard to practice intercessory prayer because, even when they believe in God and God's sovereign power, they are apt to think of God as too great to make any changes in response to our prayers. After all, does not God have basic policies? Why should God interfere just because we pray for others? In any event, is not God too great to deal in the small details concerning human beings?

In response, we must note at the outset that everything depends on whether, and to what extent, God cares for each human being. God has revealed in Jesus Christ the Ultimate One, who cares supremely for each person. And since it is God's holy plan to work through human beings in expressing ultimate compassion, God works through our prayers to bless others. The greater our God, the more God knows and loves each of us. And the greater our God, the more eager God is to summon us to prayers in behalf of our fellow human beings in need.

God's Choice to Use Us

Another objection to intercessory prayer is that God already knows every human need and, since God desires our good, our prayers are not needed. For God will already do what needs to be done without our prayers. For example, if a person is seriously ill, God already wants to heal and restore. Our prayer does nothing that God is not already doing. But the trouble with this is that it overlooks God's revealed plan to bring in the Kingdom by involving us in the process. God works through our hands and feet, through our hearts and wills, through our thoughts and minds, and through our purposes. God also works through our prayers on behalf of our fellow human beings. This implies that there are some things that will not happen without our participation. Therefore, God is continuously calling us to the kind of intercessory prayer which leads to action.

Our persistent prayers for others is driven by the evidence that God answers prayer.

Does not intercessory prayer infringe on the privacy and freedom of others? Should God tamper with a person's right to live his or her own life? When we pray for others, are we not assuming that God should override their freedom? For example, when we pray for a friend or enemy to be converted, does not this imply that we have no respect for the other's freedom to decide for himself or herself? For if God answers our prayer by converting the other person, what happens to personal freedom? In response to this, there is nothing about intercessory prayer which violates anyone's privacy or personal freedom. I may influence you, and you may influence me without any diminution of our freedom of choice. The plain fact is that we are all influenced by many forces external to ourselves. Nature influences us. Other people–including bad companions–influence us. Events influence us. The fact that, through prayer, God may influence us and others cannot be used as a sound basis for denying human freedom. We need all the good influences which God graciously gives us through the prayers of God's people.

Our Heritage of Intercession

When we turn to the great characters of the Bible, we find that nearly all of them believed in intercessory prayer. And they practiced it. In addition to Abraham, Moses, David, and the prophets, Jesus taught it and practiced it. The entire life and work of Jesus was a prayerful ministry of intercession. And, as we have already seen, next to our blessed Lord, Paul was the master exponent of the principle of intercession in prayer. Moreover, the outstanding personalities in the Christian heritage, almost without exception, were people who practiced intercessory prayer. Indeed, one of their most notable traits was their passion for the wellbeing of the souls and bodies of others which they expressed in prayer.

How can we explain the insistence of the biblical characters on intercessory prayer? And how can we account for the persistence of Christians in all eras in the practice of it? The basic answer to these questions is that people of faith have witnessed and experienced God's actions. They have seen the cumulative evidences of God's responses to their prayers for others. Here we enter into a realm of mystery. We do not know much about the laws of divine healing. But we do know that God can and does heal people both physically and spiritually. We do not know precisely how God can assist a person through the Holy Spirit in being converted and, at the same time, not tamper with his or her freedom. But we know that God does it. Our own life on this strange little planet is a mystery, but we live it.

Our prayers tap into the dimension of God's redeeming, recreating, and healing grace.

There are many things about ourselves that we do not understand. For example, the mysterious influences of the human mind upon bodily illnesses—despite scientific advances in studies of the brain—are still like unexplored terrain. Moving beyond these mind-body relationships, when we consider the reality of the personal God who knows and loves us, we may begin to open our minds to the healing and recreating work of God's grace. The least we can do in the face of doubt is to maintain an openness to the possibilities and to the witnesses of God's mysterious interaction with us in making us whole.

Entering a New Dimension

Against this background, I see no adequate basis for giving up a strong faith in the efficacy of intercessory prayer. The laws of nature abide unchanged. When we pray for others, and when God answers our prayer, no known laws of nature are suspended. Rather, what happens is that the laws of interpersonal relations are brought into operation upon our human situation. That is, another dimension of God's energies is at work. This is the dimension of God's redeeming, recreating, and healing grace. The Christian claim is that in intercessory prayer some of the mysterious depths of divine power are released and made available to people.

But if God knows our needs and wants our best interests, why should we have to pray for others? Because God withholds some ranges of grace and power until we fulfill certain conditions. Why? Because it is God's holy purpose, in his dealings with us, to work in and through us. To be sure, in many ways God takes the initiative to bless us without any effort on our part. Jesus even reminded us:

> **For he makes his sun rise on the evil and on the good, and sends rain on the righteous and on the unrighteous.**
> **Matthew 5:45 NLT**

God creates and sustains us by providential care. But the point is that over and beyond these benefits, we are also blessed through the intimate concern and involvement with each other and with God. These are the unique values and resources that come only as we are consciously and deeply related to each other in the love of Christ.

Inherent to Our Faith

To pray for one another is, in fact, inherent in who we are as a community of faith. In commissioning the believers before his death, Jesus prayed for his disciples:

> *I am not asking you to take them out of the world, but I ask you to protect them from the evil one. I ask not only on behalf of these, but also on behalf of those who will believe in me through their word, that they may all be one. As you, Father, are in me and I am in you, may they also be in us, so that the world may believe that you have sent me.*
>
> John 17: 15, 20-21 NRSV

Likewise, the early church prayed for one another anytime there was need:

> *When they had prayed, the place in which they were gathered together was shaken; and they were all filled with the Holy Spirit and spoke the word of God with boldness.*
>
> Acts 4:31 NRSV

God wants the homeless to live in good houses. God knows that they need them. But God does not build houses for them. God works through people to realize the divine purpose that they be well housed. God wants peace on earth. But God does not bring peace unless people get together and work out their differences. In all that affects our human situation, God works through our minds, our words, our prayers, and our deeds. It is a law of the spiritual realm that God will not do for us what God expects us to do with divine assistance.

Driven by Compassion

Another consideration here is that when we truly see and feel the need of others who are in misery, we can not help but pray for them. When loved ones get life threatening diseases, we cannot help praying for them. When those we love miss the way, and miss their opportunities, we cannot help but pray for them. When we begin to understand the awesome possibilities of massive destruction, we cannot help but pray for those world leaders who hold in their hands the possibilities of war and peace. When we know that the church is in a sinful world, and, in many places, is suffering persecution, and even yet, persecuting one another, we cannot help praying for the Body of Christ. What is behind this driving spiritual force moving us into intercessory prayer? Surely the answer is the Great Heart of God who wants us to be bound to each other through the mysterious ties of intercessory prayer.

Intercessory prayer binds us to each other in love. It is a marvelous source of basic good will toward others. Praying for each other connects us at a deep interpersonal level that bridges many barriers including miles. For instance, when I was a student in Boston–far from my family in Korea–I felt connected to them because I knew I was being prayed for by them. Moreover, it is the Christian conviction that God changes people and events through intercessory prayer. What is to stand in the way of divine-human interaction whereby every sincere prayer of intercession is answered through the transmission of divine suggestions and impulses? If God can put a thought into the mind of a person, God can answer prayer. If God can influence another by suggestions awakened through our prayers, God can answer those prayers. Similarly, if God, through our earnest and sincere concern for the physical health of another person, can release new spiritual and physical energies which affect his or her body, God can heal that person through our prayers. Undoubtedly these things have happened again and again.

Engaging the Mysterious

Some words of caution are needed here. We are discussing things mysterious. We do not know the laws of God's interaction with us in the interpersonal processes of praying for each other. We only know that in these processes we meet reality. We do not know the laws of divine healing. We affirm that God can heal anyone of any disease, and we affirm that all healing comes from God. God works through physicians, surgeons, nurses, hospitals and through the patients themselves to heal. God works through changes in climate and physical environments to heal. God heals through changes in the attitudes of people, and God works through the prayers of caring people to heal. Biblical history and Christian history are filled with stories of individuals being healed which occurred because of prayer. The following words of Scripture give witness to what has happened:

> *The earnest prayer of a righteous person has great power and wonderful results.*
>
> **James 5:16 NLT**

It is with good reason, based on Scripture and experience, that pastors and congregations of all Christian churches pray earnestly for the sick and dying.

We know that many of us will become sick, and that all of us will someday die. But we cannot believe that God wants anyone to die without our prayers. And we know that God does not want any human being to die prematurely. Therefore, we shall continue to pray for God's healing presence and power to restore the sick to health. We know that in many cases, despite all our prayers, the diseases continue steadily on their courses until even some of God's best children die prematurely. Nevertheless, we believe it is God's holy will for us to pray for healing of body and spirit; and we leave the rest to God.

Intercessory prayer, therefore, is what we do trusting the rest to God. In doing so, God enriches us through intercessory prayer in the following ways. First, God gives all the desires of our heart that we experience from a closer walk with our Creator which binds us to God.

Second, through intercessory prayer, God quickens and enlarges the love of neighbor and thus binds us closer to each other.

Third, when we pray for others in the spirit of Christ, we act to bring about the good we pray for. As a result of our own prayers, we serve others. So when we pray for God to heal another, we try to find ways in which we can help in the healing process. When we pray for a person to be converted, we try to do what we can to draw that person into the understanding of the love of Christ.

And fourth, through intercessory prayer, God releases energies which would otherwise be withheld. When we intercede in prayer for others, we submit ourselves to become open channels of God's transforming grace and love for others.

Perhaps now we can understand better why God summons us to pray for each other and for the needs of the whole world. Jesus said:

> *The harvest is plentiful, but the laborers are few; therefore ask the Lord of the harvest to send out laborers into his harvest.*
>
> **Matthew 9:37-38 NRSV**

147

Questions for Reflection

1. In many ways, praying for others is an ultimate act of faith in that we pray trusting God to act in the other's life. When have you, by faith, interceded for someone else trusting that God would act when all "evidence" might have told you otherwise?

2. When have you experienced the collective power of the community of faith praying for you?

3. When has God placed on your heart the compassion and desire to pray for someone who you later realized really needed it?

4. When have you been moved to action through your prayers for another?

person-to-Person Connection

God, through the Holy Spirit, will at times "cause us" to pray for someone else by bringing them to mind.

The next time someone is clearly–and maybe unexpectedly–brought to mind for you, take time to stop and specifically pray for them. Write them a note or give them a call to let them know how you were convicted to pray for them.

Fourteen

Prayer and the Meaning of Life

In moments of prayer we have direct experiences of the meaning and glory of life. For in prayer we know that God is with us, that God cares, and that what we think and do really matters. In prayer, then, the whole sweep of revealed religion becomes an experienced reality, through this Divine-human encounter in the midst of our day-to-day lives.

One of the deepest and most insistent questions we ask is this: does life have any enduring meaning? This question is often asked in relation to death. In that case, the question takes one of the following forms: What is the meaning of life in the face of a sure death? If at death we end up at zero, how can we make sense out of our lives? What difference does anything make in the end?

Across many centuries some of the greatest thinkers have devoted long and painful hours to these questions. Some have said that life is absurd, meaningless, without any enduring significance. Others have insisted that each human life has meaning both in itself and, more basically, in relation to God's revealed purpose for us.

It was one of the tragedies of the twentieth century that, as it moved from decade to decade, it failed to produce many strong philosophical minds who support the idea that human life has enduring meaning and glory. Consequently, we may say with regret that many of the philosophers of our time have offered very little help on this important issue. It strikes me as completely unsatisfying to believe with what is known as process theology that our only enduring meaning is in our contribution to God's enrichment. In that perspective, we have no enduring selfhood, no soul which can pass beyond death into eternal life. The sacred line of self-identity is obliterated at death. Where then is the enduring meaning of our souls?

On this theme the philosophers known as Personalists have more to offer than any others. According to the Personalists, God is a personal God who is the only ultimate reality and each human being is a person with individual worth in God's sight and divine purpose. This view is firmly reflected in the Bible where God is the personal God who knows us, loves us, redeems us, and communes with us. And we are creatures of unutterable worth. For we were created by God to exist as living individual souls with the power to think, feel, and act.

Finding Meaning at the Cross

At a meeting of the American Philosophical Association several years ago, one session was devoted to "the meaning of life." It attracted wide interest. Many of the philosophers from the eastern colleges and universities in the United States were there. And nearly all of them attended this plenary session. The main lecture was delivered by a philosopher from Princeton University. He developed the ancient theme that our life has no enduring meaning. By prearrangement two philosophers responded as critics. One of these, a philosopher from Harvard University, urged that, on the contrary, life has meaning. We experience this, he said. We know that it does matter as to whether we do a just or unjust act. But even the

Harvard philosopher concluded by suggesting that in the end life has little meaning. "For," he said, "if God is, I would expect him to take an unexcited view of man."

As scores of the philosophers laughed, I thought of the whole sweep of revealed religion. I thought of the prophets who reminded the people of Israel of God's concern for them in God's covenantal relationship. I thought of Jesus Christ and his passion for one of the least. I thought of the vast Christian movement with its prayers, hymns, sacraments, symbols, preaching, devotional services, and its saints. Then I said to myself, "That's it! The essence of Christianity–on one side of it–is precisely that God takes an excited view of each human being." So, while we may sit at the feet of philosophers and learn a few things, we kneel at the foot of the Cross and celebrate! Celebrate what? The mysterious, glorious fact that the infinite God of this universe who created each one of us for an enduring meaning. What could not be discovered by our reason has been revealed in God's Word. And this revelation becomes an experienced reality when God meets us in prayer.

We can sit with philosophers and learn a few things, but we kneel at the foot of the Cross and celebrate! Our lives matter supremely!

Revealed in the Word

The biblical revelation, from one standpoint, is a vast succession of events and utterances on the dignity, meaning,

and glory of human life under God. It never lapses into
the arrogant and degrading notion that we can be or do
anything apart from God. But it constantly urges that our life
is important to God, that God cares about the way we live,
and that God wants us to work by grace in the realization
of values. Where else can we go to understand the vast
importance of humans on earth? Not to biology or to any
other science. Only in the biblical revelation from Genesis to
Revelation, with Christ at its center, can we find the unique
and supreme importance of human beings in the sight of
God. That is, the Bible is a vast and inspired summons to join
with God in doing a great work in the Kingdom. Jesus taught
this clearly, simply, and profoundly.

The Christian communities of prayer and faith, for all their
imperfections, are divinely inspired media for telling the good
news of this biblical affirmation of the meaning and dignity
of each human being. The very thought, made explicit in
preaching, teaching, singing, praying, and serving others, that
God cared enough to give Jesus Christ on our behalf tells the
story. God takes an excited view of each human being.

> *While we were still sinners, Christ died for us.*
> **Romans 5:8 NIV**

An understanding of the meaning and preciousness of our
souls comes home to each of us in prayer. Here we know that
God is with us in all that we are and do. No matter what our
failures and weaknesses may be, we are assured in prayer by
the inner witness that God's love is real, and our love speaking
and for our fellow human beings is important.

Experienced in Worship and Prayer

In prayer and worship we have the only concrete experience

152

of the enduring meaning of our lives on earth. Here we pass from the theoretical to the practical, from thought to life. Surely one of the most important motives for praying and worshiping is to experience for ourselves the peace and joy of knowing that what we are and do matters. For in worship and prayer, God is with us, delights in us, and empowers us for service and in service. The significance of a vital prayer-life for experiencing the sense of life's enduring meaning cannot be exaggerated. Intellectual reflection helps us to ground our faith rationally, but life is so much deeper than logic. What the Bible reveals about God's work in us is confirmed in our ongoing experiences in prayer and worship.

The ultimate meaning of our lives as humans only becomes real in prayer.

To understand the importance of prayer to the meaning of life, we must affirm four things. First: God exists and cares for each human being. Without this certainty there is no ultimate basis for hope or meaning in our passing careers or time on earth. Prayer changes this basic tenet from a merely intellectual affirmation into an experienced reality. God's choice to engage with us in this Divine-human encounter of prayer affirms that God cares for each of us dearly.

The second foundational affirmation is this: The God who created and sustains the universe has revealed divine love for each person through Jesus Christ, the Son of God, who lived, died, and was raised from the dead that all might have everlasting life. This revelation could not have been made with such power, beauty, and sublimity by words alone. Therefore, God took the initiative in Jesus Christ, the Living Word, to make known that unalterable love for us. This too becomes personally real in our hearts through prayer. It was in worship, prayer and bible study that John Wesley experienced his "strange warming of the heart" that let him know Jesus Christ did die for him.

The third foundational affirmation essential to the Christian understanding of the meaning of life is that each human being is a soul created in the image of God and made for an everlasting destiny.

> *So God created people in his own image; God patterned them after himself; male and female he created them. God blessed them and told them, "Multiply and fill the earth and subdue it. Be masters over the fish and birds and all the animals."*
> **Genesis 1:27-28 NLT**

There are many modern perspectives on our human nature which argue that humans are reduced to mere chemical processes or to brain processes or to that which is merely physical. A human being is not merely an animal among animals–the fortuitous product of blind chance. A human being is a living body and soul made for an everlasting destiny with God. One would think that the most capable minds in the world would be doing everything they could, with solid reasons, to show the preciousness and dignity of each human being. But this would not be possible by any theory which reduces the soul to something physical. No, the reality of our ultimate meaning as humans can never be reduced–nor even explained in merely physical processes.

Only of us as humans is it said that by God's act of creation human beings alone are created in the image of God. And only of humans does the Bible say:

> *For you made us only a little lower than God, and you crowned us with glory and honor.*
>
> **Psalm 8:5 NLT**

The great laboratory of the human world is open not only to notable psychologists and other scholars. It is a realm where all human beings are witnesses because they deal daily in interpersonal relations on the assumption that each is a conscious being, that each is characterized by selfhood, self-identity, personality and responsibility. What the Bible affirms, our wisest introspection and common sense, world-wide, civilization-wide, race-wide, and gender-wide supports. For example, only human beings speak, understand, read, write and communicate through languages in sentences, paragraphs and books. Dogs bark, cats meow, lambs bleat, horses whinny, birds chatter, lions growl, and the big apes grunt and make other sounds, but none of the other animals speak in languages as do all races of human beings.

What makes humans "religious" is that we seek out a Divine-human relationship in asking the great questions.

All this, when elaborated, tells in library-sized mountains of data about how vastly different the human species is from all other species. To be sure, many other creatures breathe the same air we do, drink the same waters, eat similar foods, move about on the same earth, see and hear the same objects as we do, and die with us. But, we as humans are far more than physical beings. The brain is a physical thing. It has weight, can be measured and located in space and be probed, photographed, scanned and x-rayed. Consciousness, or more particularly, my consciousness, cannot be found in space. It cannot be x-rayed. Does that mean that I do not exist as a person or mind or soul? Of course not. For that would deny the common sense of people world-wide, race-wide and gender-wide. It would make biographies impossible. For historians know that all recorded events in biographies are traced back to personal agents. Much more could come from hearing those in the arts, in commerce, law, medicine, philosophy and religion. The reason no other creatures are religious is not that they are atheists, but that they have no interest in asking the great questions pertaining to life, death, sins and destiny.

The fourth foundational affirmation essential to the Christian understanding of the meaning of life is that when our present bodies die, our souls live on. The human soul is not its body or any part of its body. These two, body and soul (or mind), are intimately and causally interrelated. The soul affects the body and the body the soul. But they are distinct realities. Therefore, when the body has served its purpose and dies, this does not mean the death of the soul. The God who in this life made possible the marvelous interconnections between our souls and bodies can certainly ensure the soul's pilgrimage in the life to come. Everything here depends on God's holy purpose for us. God has revealed this in the resurrection of Jesus. And we experience in prayer the unbreakable bonds of God's love that even in death, can not be broken. In prayer we are assured of the everlasting adventures in God's heavenly kingdom.

Questions for Reflection

1. How and when have you tried to find purpose or meaning for your life?

2. How have you found meaning for your life in God's Word? In worship? In prayer?

3. When have you been assured of God's purpose or meaning for you during times of prayer?

person-to-Person Connection

Read Psalm 139 and insert your own name—reading it out loud as prayer in conversation with God. Then allow God to respond to you in prayer affirming God's divine presence with you, thoughts about you and plans for you.

Write down or journal what God may be speaking to you in this Psalm.

Fifteen

Prayer and Faith

Faith, hope, and love are the three abiding Christian virtues. Many things come and go, but faith abides as we find in the famous thirteenth chapter of First Corinthians. Therefore, faith is a key word in the vocabulary of every Christian, and faith is a foundational word in all of Scripture. In the New Testament, in particular, this word expresses what is at the heart of our soul's salvation in our person-to-Person relationship with God.

What is faith? It is putting our absolute trust in God's pardoning, redeeming, and recreating power in Jesus Christ. On our side, faith means bringing our whole being, with the help of the Holy Spirit, to the experience of absolute confidence and trust in God's power to save, keep, and recreate us after the likeness of Christ. So the word "faith" here belongs not in the arena of general culture, but in the unique dimension of the religious and in particular, the Christian life.

In Whom Do We Trust?

I have often heard people say that we must have faith to live at all. We have faith that the air we breathe is not contaminated with destructive gases. We have faith that our food, prepared unseen by us, is not poisoned. We have faith that the sidewalks will not roll up and hit us in the face. We have faith in the laws of nature and of human nature. And so it goes. However, when we think only in these lesser terms, we are sure to be shutting ourselves from the realm of faith as understood by Jesus and the apostles.

Why? Because having faith in nature and human beings, though indispensable, does not come to grips with our moral and spiritual need to trust in something far greater than ourselves. This "animal faith" is not the doorway to the forgiveness of our sins, nor do we receive from it the power over temptation. We can have limited trust in the best elements of civilization and culture but this kind of faith does not and cannot take us into the life-giving relationship with God. The real issues of our souls—the struggles with sin, mediocrity, selfishness, loss of morale, indifference, anxiety and dread, tragedy and sorrow, meaninglessness and emptiness—are left unanswered by faith in nature and civilization.

> **But where sin increased,
> grace abounded all the more.**
> **Romans 5:20 NLT**

For this reason Paul distinguishes clearly between putting our trust in the offerings of this world and holding fast to God. Regarding this supreme faith, Paul said: *for we walk by faith, not by sight* (Second Corinthians 5:7). What does this mean? It means that we do not place our ultimate trust in the things we can see, or taste, or handle, or in anything that is, merely human. Instead, our supreme faith is in God alone.

Paul affirms that we must hold fast to the infinite goodness of God in Jesus Christ no matter what we have done, where we have been, or who we are. We are to trust God to pardon us and to pardon us absolutely.

For *where sin increased, grace abounded all the more* we are told in Romans 5:20. We are to hold fast to God for the courage and power to see life through. We are to trust God to help us in all creative and worthy endeavors. And above all we are to trust God to bring us into a living relationship with our Maker and Redeemer through his Son, Jesus Christ and the work of the Holy Spirit. Augustine summarized all this when he said, *I have learned, above all things, never to make man the foundation of my trust.* But such faith does not come easily. It comes out of the agonies of struggle, doubt, heartbreak, desperation. More deeply, it comes when the Holy Spirit moves in our souls as we pray. Paul knew this when he said,

> *Likewise the Spirit helps us in our weakness; for we do not know how to pray as we ought, but that very Spirit intercedes with sighs too deep for words.*
> **Romans 8:26 NRSV**

Suppose our problem is that we are sinners as we all are. We know it. Those who love us know it. God knows it. We feel that we are too unworthy to be saved at all by God. We feel that we cannot be forgiven because we are too unworthy to be considered for any benefit from God. When strong souls feel this way, they are apt to start doing good works. They get busy and try to whip up some merit before God by their deeds. But those who persist in this error end up saying with Martin Luther, who tried to work his way into God's favor, *Nor would my conscience, even if I should live and work to all eternity, ever come to a settled certainty, how much it ought to do in order to satisfy God.* He never saw the Light until he read with new insight these momentous words in Romans 1:17.

It is through faith that a righteous person has life.

Only such faith breaks the chains of our self-righteousness and frees us from the bondage of trying to prove our worth to move into the new life of true righteousness which only comes through a relationship with God.

No words can exaggerate the importance of faith in bringing God and us together. Here we are not dealing in mere intellectual reflection which–though important in its special function–has no power to save. Nor are we concerned with mere forms and ceremonies which, apart from faith, have no power to redeem or recreate. Nor are we referring to hard work, sacrifices, self-discipline, or moral duty, which, though having their proper roles, do not and cannot function to bring us to God. Even our willingness to repent and surrender ourselves to God falls dead without faith. Repentance and surrender are necessary. But the power of God comes by grace through faith. When we repent and hold fast to God's mighty action in Jesus Christ on our behalf, we are forgiven. Similarly, when we put our trust in God, we are conquerors over temptation. When we trust God to help us in a great cause for others, we receive God's power, which enriches and enhances our otherwise feeble resources. Through faith God empowers us both for mission and in mission.

These abundant blessings of faith become available primarily through prayer. For in vital prayer the soul ceases its merely intellectual, aesthetic, moral, ritualistic approaches and gets down to the essential process of opening itself to God. In prayer, commitment is basic, and in authentic prayer the whole person (thought, feeling, will, desires and aims) is brought before God. And by the mysterious movements of the Holy Spirit, the soul is aided until it can take the leap of faith of absolute trust in God's forgiving and empowering love in Jesus Christ. Then begins the new dimension of existence with God. All of this comes into being in the life of prayer where faith is born and nurtured. When we pray, faith thrives. When we stop praying, faith shrivels up and dies.

Therefore, through prayer we join the inspired writer of Hebrews who said:

> *So, you see, it is impossible to please God without faith. Anyone who wants to come to him must believe that there is a God and that he rewards those who sincerely seek him.*
> **Hebrews 11:6 NLT**

When we pray, faith thrives. When we stop praying, faith shrivels up and dies.

Questions for Reflection

1. In what "things" or entities do we place our trust? How is faith in God remarkably different?

2. How and when do we try and prove our worth and what is its effect on us?

3. When has prayer opened you up to God's redeeming, restoring, and renewing grace at work in you by faith, or trust, that God would do so?

person-to-Person Connection

Think of an area in your life where you have tried by your own might, or by relying on the might of others, to make things right.

Lift that area of your life in prayer submitting your own might to the power that only comes from God.

Sixteen

Prayer and Hope

Hope is the second of the three abiding Christian virtues, and in the New Testament it is given an emphasis unique in the history of religion. Christianity is a religion of faith and love, but it is also a religion of hope. As in all of its major teachings, the roots of the Christian understanding of hope go back to the Old Testament, where the psalmists put their hope in God's faithfulness or steadfast love which endures for ever

> *O give thanks to the Lord, for he is good;*
> *for his steadfast love endures forever.*
> **Psalm 106:1 NRSV**

What is hope? It is the confident expectation of something marvelous in the future. It is the anticipated Kingdom of God yet to come. In the Christian understanding, hope includes the desire for a worthwhile life for all people, as far as possible on earth, and also for a glorious life with God in heaven. So there are really two levels of Christian hope. One is the hope for a better life on earth. The other is the hope for a marvelous life in that new realm that we call the Kingdom of Heaven.

Hope for Our Future

Here, I shall consider primarily the way prayer affects our whole attitude toward the future on earth. In a later chapter I shall treat the theme of prayer and the hope of heaven. What I have in mind here, then, concerns whether optimism about the future is based on reality.

The battle between optimism and pessimism has been fought in every society and in every soul. No one can escape this issue and, more than that, this personal struggle. Sometimes this struggle between hope and despair involves encounters with fatalism or the belief we can do nothing about the future. There are environmental fatalisms, genetic or biological fatalisms, psychological fatalisms, and other sophisticated fatalisms. However contemporary they may seem, their advocates join their ancient forebears in crying out as the bones in Ezekiel's valley, "We are all dried up. Our hope is all gone." But long after these fatalisms have come and gone, the story of the prodigal son, the glory of the Cross and Resurrection, and the miracle of Pentecost will remain to give hope to all who experience in prayer the power of God in Jesus Christ. When we think about the problem of fatalism and despair, we see that without God there is no enduring basis for hope. So when we leave God out of our lives, we place ourselves within the prison walls of an unremitting despair. To be without hope is to be *without God in the world* (Ephesians 2:12).

Without God, there is no enduring basis for hope.

Thirsting for Hope in a Dreary Land

Tolstoy, the Russian novelist, saw this. At a time when outwardly everything seemed to be going his way when his wife loved him, his children respected him, his friends and relatives honored him, and the world applauded him, he fell into a profound despair. He could not understand how the peasants could sing or anyone be happy. By his own testimony he had someone hide the rope lest he tie himself to the rafters. He refused to go hunting lest he turn the gun on himself. As Joseph Fort Newton has put it, "He was a man going and not arriving, seeking and not finding; he was a God-haunted man." Tolstoy himself spoke of his experience as "a thirst for God." After two long agonizing years of searching, Tolstoy said, "God is that one without whom we cannot live."

We are like fish in ever-shallowing waters. We are like fish cast upon the shore beating out their life on the sands of an alien world. Then, if after all the futile flapping, one of them makes a final desperate lunge toward the sea, it finds an answering response in the element that gave it life. The psalmist expresses this desperate longing in these words:

> *As a deer longs for flowing streams, so my soul longs for you, O God. My soul thirsts for God, for the living God. When shall I come and behold the face of God?*
> Psalm 42:1-2 NIV

Life is deeper and more important than thought. It must be rooted in relationship.

On one side, the quest for hope must have intellectual foundation. For much depends on our total world-view. If we believe that nature (the physical universe) is ultimate, the best we can do is to take refuge in heroic efforts and despair because ultimately we shall be crushed under the trampling march of unconscious power.

But, when we believe in God, who is made known in the Bible, and who is affirmed by our best thinking, and experience, the theological foundation for hope has been firmly laid.

Overcoming Despair

The practical basis for hope cannot be established only theologically. Even when we believe in God but do not enter into the life-giving faith-relationship with God, we merely overcome despair intellectually but not spiritually. Life is deeper and more important than thought. Therefore, we require both the theological and the practical answers to the problem of unremitting despair. How can this practical answer be found? In the Bible it is found through prayer and faith. This is more easily stated than experienced. For we are faced here with a persistent and dangerously destructive force in our lives. Pessimism is the swindling voice of Satan urging us to give up our highest hopes and ideals and give in to our lesser natures. Nevertheless, through prayer and faith our deepest despair can be conquered. It can be defeated only when we enter and continuously reenter the faith relationship

We must employ the heart principle of the devotional life: In returning shall be your strength.

with the living Christ who is greater than all possible causes of discouragement.

But let us never be deceived into supposing that there is a one-time, one-moment solution to any serious form of pessimism or despair. Just when we feel free from its clutches, the demonic voice whispers in our ears thoughts of gloom and defeat. Therefore, we must employ the heart-principle of the devotional life: In returning shall be your strength. That is, we must return again and again to the Source of spiritual power and renewal, namely, the living Christ.

Our pessimistic moods are often brought on by our physical condition, body chemistry, loss of sleep, stress, sickness, and other physical factors. Or, these moods may come from psychological pressures. These moods may have their source in the attitudes and actions of other people, or they may result from catastrophic events which drain away all hope. More deeply and pervasively, unremitting despair may come from sin, wrong living, and the guilt that blinds us to the God of love, mercy, and hope.

Whatever shakes the foundations of our whole being must be faced. For the person who prays persistently and in faith, God is known to be the One who is immeasurably greater than all the forces threatening our very existence. Our prayers thus bind us to God and provide the hope we need privately and communally. For to overcome pessimism and to live in hope, we need to share in the sustaining prayers of the community of faith.

Hope for Triumphant Victory

Moreover, through our prayers that bind us to God, we have the only sustaining basis for the ultimate triumph of righteousness. The Christian faith satisfies this profound yearning. Throughout the Bible and in prayer, God is revealed as the One who has already made provision for the triumph of righteousness. The cross is followed by the Resurrection, the crucifix by the sign of the cross. Therefore, in those who pray in faith there is a present assurance of victory. For God is with us, and we will ultimately and eternally be with God.

A faithful Christian is undiscourageable. This is not to suggest that we may not have our pessimistic moments. It is rather to affirm that through prayer in faith we overcome these moments by the unbreakable bonds with the God and Father of our Lord Jesus Christ. God does not create and sustain a magnificent universe and human beings capable of becoming bearers of the divine grace and then allow everything to fizzle out in the end. Degeneration cannot get the last word in God's universe.

Therefore, we join the ancient psalmists in saying that the steadfast love of God endures forever. With the angel Gabriel we too sing of the Messiah, saying, "Of his kingdom there will be no end" (Luke 1:33). And we join the loud voices in heaven in proclaiming:

> *The kingdom of the world has become the kingdom of our Lord and of his Christ, and he will reign for ever and ever.*
> **Revelation 11:15 NIV**

Questions for Reflection

1. When have you been overcome with pessimism or despair? How were your prayers (or the prayers of others) instrumental in delivering you from that despair?

2. When has the voice of the enemy tried to convince you to give up on a hope that God instilled in your heart?

3. When have the prayers of the community of faith given you hope when you otherwise had none?

person-to-Person Connection

The next time you hear the "whisper of the enemy" try to convince you to give up on what God has set before you, pray repeatedly in faith and hope this paraphrased prayer from Romans 8:37:

No! Overwhelming victory is mine through Christ Jesus who loves me!

Seventeen
Prayer and Love

It is a self-evident truth of psychiatry that we may truly live, if we truly love. This is to reaffirm what Jesus lived and taught nearly two thousand years ago. Love is the royal law of life. It is foundational in being a real person. And it is at the heart of our existence in the world as Christians. In this chapter we shall see that there have always been deep-rooted obstacles, both in human nature and in human civilizations, that have blocked the way to Christian love. This leads us to approach prayer in the name of Christ as the divinely appointed way to Christian love.

First, let's look at love itself. What is this love? It is not merely human affection, and it goes beyond our self-understanding. In order to see what it is, we require God's self-revelation as love. And the divine summons to love may be heard first through the Old Testament where God calls people to holiness. God commands Moses to say to the people:

> *Say this to the entire community of Israel: You must be holy because I, the Lord your God, am holy.*
>
> **Leviticus 19:1-2 NLT**

This call to the whole community of Israel became what is called the holiness code. It is detailed in a long series of laws found in Leviticus 18-26. The idea of the holiness code was taken up by the earliest Christians, who understood the meaning of holiness from the perspective of God's revelation in Christ. So, holiness is Christian love through Christ at work in us for the glory of God and the blessing of others.

For it is written, "You shall be holy, for I am holy." If you invoke as Father the one who judges all people impartially according to their deeds, live in reverent fear during the time of your exile. You know that you were ransomed from the futile ways inherited from your ancestors, not with perishable things like silver or gold, but with the precious blood of Christ, like that of a lamb without defect or blemish. He was destined before the foundation of the world, but was revealed at the end of the ages for your sake. Through him you have come to trust in God, who raised him from the dead and gave him glory, so that your faith and hope are set on God.

First Peter 1:16-21 NRSV

The Life of Love

There are three decisive reasons why Christians hear God's call to live the life of love. First, God is love and therefore God requires us to live according to the divine purpose. The God of holy love gives the two great commandments:

"Love the Lord your God with all your heart and with all your soul and with all your mind." This is the first and greatest commandment.

And the second is like it: "Love your neighbor as yourself." All the Law and the Prophets hang on these two commandments.

Matthew 22.37-40 NIV

Jesus was quoting from Deuteronomy 6:5 and Leviticus 19:18. These two verses would be well known to his listeners that day.

Second, by his teaching and example, Jesus calls us to love. He manifested this call supremely on the cross when he gave himself that all who believe might have everlasting life.

Third, life demands love. No one can truly live without it. For God created our human nature—with all of its levels and varieties—for love.

We pray for God's grace to live the life of love.

But we cannot weave into our daily living the love of Christ without God's help. Therefore, we are to hear the divine summons to pray for the grace to live the life of love. We are to pray in faith, confidently; for we know that the God who commands us to love has promised with that command the grace to realize it. Therefore, when we go to God in prayer, we know that God is present to quicken our own resolve and to help us to make real the love of God and neighbor. In this way we can carry out our Lord's summons to:

> *Let your good deeds shine out for all to see, so that everyone will praise your heavenly Father.*
>
> **Matthew 5:16 NLT**

Why Prayer is Required

The reason why earnest prayer is required for the life of Christian love is that it is not easy to love and to be loved. Again and again, we find ourselves lapsing into a disease of the soul which has characterized all civilizations, namely, the sin of looking down on others and consequently trampling upon them. The theme song of this awesome evil force in us is: "I'm up here and you're down there, and don't you ever forget it." All communities have been and are corrupted by it. It is one of the surest signs of our human depravity. It, together with the pride and greed which it implies, is the primary source of tyranny and oppression. Consequently, it inevitably brings on the awful scourge of "man's inhumanity to man."

This sense of egotistic superiority of status carries with it the conviction that it is right to trample upon others. This is the primary driving force of racial prejudice. In many nations across the centuries where women have been belittled and "kept in their place" this sense of superiority was the major cause of the exploitation of girls and women. Augustine refers to:

> **that notorious law...which prohibited a man from making a woman, even an only daughter, his heir; which law I am at a loss to conceive what could be more unjust.**

But, bad as that was, it was trivial compared to the brutalities meted out to women and children around the world.

A documentary on justice in Brazil showed how, in some cases, husbands who murdered their wives have admitted their guilt and gone free. Why? Because the juries considered the supposed violation of the "honor" of the husbands as more important than the wives whom they murdered. No nations or societies are free from the injustices and brutalities which crush the souls and bodies of human beings for whom Christ died.

It is self-evident that there are vast ranges of inequality among human beings. We are not equal in talents, abilities, skills, self-discipline, physical strength, emotions, and will. Every father, mother, and teacher knows this. Nor are we equal in the privileges of birth and fortune. This elemental fact of life is a source of enjoyment and entertainment for people on all levels of life and ability. Regardless of our skills, position, and influence, we enjoy seeing, reading, and hearing the results of the achievements of outstanding persons. The masses applaud the performances of the stars. And all who can, seek out and pay for the services of great physicians, teachers, statesmen, writers, artists, composers, and athletes. All applaud those leaders of business and industry who develop successful enterprises which employ thousands of people and put bread on their tables. And many are those who appreciate unusually gifted preachers.

But does this vast diversity of talents, skills, education, achievements–this extensive inequality among human beings–entitle anyone to look down on others or to trample upon them? Of course not. Augustine continues to state his profound conviction:

> *No man has a right to lead such a life of contemplation as to forget in his own ease the service due to his neighbor; nor has any man a right to be so immersed in active life as to neglect the contemplation of God.... And, in active life, it is not the honors or power of this life we should covet...but we should aim at using our position and influence, if we have been honorably attained, for the welfare of those who are under us.*

Amid all the differences among people, we are all unspeakably precious in God's sight. All of us stand in the need of prayer

175

and grace. Before the issues of life and death and destiny, we are all equal. And, at the foot of the Cross, we all kneel on the same level. People in positions of power and influence—as well as all others—need to pray for compassion. And what is Christian compassion but a feeling for others who are in misery and the desire to do what we can to help them? This is precisely what Christ brings, namely, the fellow-feeling which moves us to action. Jesus Christ came into the world to counteract the demonic forces of pride, greed, and superiority, which have been the chief sources of oppression and cruelty across the centuries.

We all kneel on the same level.

I do not think that the effects for good of our Lord's teaching on the incalculable value of each human soul have ever been adequately treated in writing. Alfred North Whitehead touches on it in the chapter entitled "The Human Soul" found in his book, *Adventures of Ideas*. There he suggests that, after centuries of slavery, the idea of the soul gradually played a decisive role in its abolition. And wherever the influence of Jesus Christ is felt, the call to human rights is heard. It was the Nazarene, more than all others put together, who gave embodiment through his followers to the mighty theme of liberation by identifying himself with "one of the least of these my brethren."

Jesus taught his followers to go against both our natural feelings and the generally accepted practices of the world in order to love the most needy. The outcasts, the lepers, the poor, the ignorant, the hated Samaritans, the sinners—all those who were in special need—were precious persons on whom he had compassion. The most difficult people to love are our enemies. In no society throughout the centuries—with some special exceptions—has love of enemies been acceptable. Yet Jesus made a special point of teaching his followers to love their enemies and pray for those who mistreated them.

Besides the love for the needy and for our enemies, Jesus taught us to learn, with God's help, to love ourselves and those dear to us. This too is not always easy. It requires God's help. It requires a lifetime of growth in understanding and affection in and throughout difficult circumstances. And it requires prayer.

God-ordained Pathway

By now it should be clear that when we speak of Christian love, we do not mean a weak, sentimental, mushy feeling or mood. On the contrary, Christian love is strong, creative, and courageous. It is the sustained desire or policy, born in us by grace, for God's best for everyone. This is never a merely human achievement. Therefore, prayer is a God-ordained pathway to Christian love. The Bible does not teach that we can love those in greatest need or love our enemies in our own strength alone. Jesus knew that we could not and would not do it. Saul of Tarsus, the great seeker after righteousness through the law, discovered that he could not be what God wanted him to be without the power of the living Christ. It was that power which enabled him to pray for his enemies, to love and care for "the saints," and to write First Corinthians 13. In the light of this, we can see why Paul gloried in Jesus Christ, through whom he became a conqueror over sin and

177

adversity.

The mighty Christian affirmation here, then, is that through prayer God meets us where we are and drives out our focus on ego, bitterness, hostility, and indifference. God does this by filling us with the mysterious, wonderful, divine love. And this love–which is the love of Christ–makes us new. Through prayer we are set on a new course in the name of Jesus Christ. We experience an almost unbelievable release from all the old fears and hostilities. And we become truly concerned for God's best for everyone, including our enemies. This does not mean that we want our enemies to have their way, whether right or wrong. That would be nonsense. Nor does it mean that we are to yield to their evil ways. That would be joining the forces of injustice and oppression. It simply means that we pray for God's best for all people.

It is no trifling matter to know by direct experience that love is the creative dynamic of life. We should never pass this by lightly. For this concerns the essence of Christianity. Paul knew it. Speaking from the heights and depths of his struggles and triumphs, he said that no matter who you are, or what you do, or what talents you have, or how much you know, or what your place in society is, if you do not have love, you are nothing. You are sounding brass or a tinkling cymbal. And nothing you do endures in the Kingdom of God. For additional clarity on this point see First Corinthians 13. Strong words! But when we think about them, we begin to get the message.

Prayer Propels to Service

What Paul was reflecting on prayerfully and what we are

wrestling with in our own souls is the phony and inauthentic in contrast to what is of utmost importance. In prayer, then, through Jesus Christ we begin the great new pilgrimage toward an authentic life of love which puts us into the center of at least some ranges of service for those in need. As for our enemies, we hate their evil ways and still love them. We no longer have time or energy to waste on hostility. So we pray for those who mistreat us, we seek God's best for them as well as for ourselves, and we go on to do all the good we can. Jesus did not stop to counsel with Judas even though he told him to his face that he was the betrayer. But he prayed for Judas as well as for the others when he said:

> *Father, forgive them; for they do not know what they are doing.*
>
> **Luke 23:34 NRSV**

I said that through Jesus Christ we enter upon "at least some ranges of service for those in need." Some people have the feeling that they ought to respond to every cry for help. But this is not possible. Some are experts at peacemaking, others at raising money for good causes, others at race relations. Some are effective at building life-serving institutions, others at creating great homes. Still others are specially gifted in witnessing and evangelizing. All Christians are called to serve, but not all are chosen for the same tasks. And though, through prayer and giving, we share in the total mission of the community of prayer, faith, and service, each has his or her own ways of concrete personal involvement in the life of service. All members are working parts of the body of Christ. And all are needed for responding compassionately to the urgent cries of human beings in misery.

The struggling stream of duty needs to be amplified by the Niagara of the grace of God.

But again, the biblical-Christian teaching is that we can do no great work of love apart from the grace of God. This is not to deny that many good deeds are performed by human beings who have not responded to the light of Christ. For all human beings are bearers of God's grace on one level or another. There is the same opportunity for everyone to see the truth.

> *The one who is the true light, who gives light to everyone.*
> **John 1:9 NLT**

The true light, which enlightens everyone, was coming into the world. But since we are concerned here with the kind of love which is so frequently pushed aside by our pride and selfishness—as well as by the paltry standards of the world around us—we require the earnest prayers for the love of Christ in order to glorify God and to be a blessing to our fellow human beings. And, with these prayers, we are to pray that God will so sustain us in all good endeavors through these words of encouragement:

> *So don't get tired of doing what is good. Don't get discouraged and give up, for we will reap a harvest of blessing at the appropriate time.*
> **Galatians 6:9 NLT**

Our prayer will be:

Help us, O God, to be imitators of Jesus Christ, to walk as he walked, to love as he loved, and to spread scriptural holiness in the Church and throughout the world.

Inward holiness that leads to outward holiness is intrinsically beautiful, intrinsically rational, and intrinsically Christ like.

Questions for Reflection

1. How or when have you experienced prayer as an "equalizer" among individuals or groups of people?

2. How has your personal regard for another person (especially an "enemy") changed when you began praying for them? Why do you think Jesus insisted that we pray for our enemies?

3. How can prayer propel us to authentic service for others? When has your service for others been affected when you intentionally prayed for those you were serving? How have you been affected when others prayed for us as the servant?

person-to-Person Connection

Identify at least one person (or group of people) which whom you have struggled to love, appreciate or be in relationship. Ask God to help you see them through God's eyes and to love them with the compassion of Christ. Pray daily that God's grace and love will be abundant in their lives.

Eighteen

Prayer and Wisdom

Among the books of the Old Testament, three are often identified as "wisdom literature." The inclusion of these in the Hebrew Bible indicates that it was a part of their heritage to give a special place to practical good sense or wisdom. Often this wisdom is in the form of maxims, or rules of conduct that express the distilled insights of experience. Gerhard von Rad likens a maxim to "a precious stone among trinkets." He says, "The demand which it must always satisfy is that of brevity, of compactness, and yet of intelligibility, with, if possible, a clear graphic quality; in short, that of being easily remembered" Some of the teachings of Jesus are in the form of maxims. In any event, the "wisdom literature," the teachings of Jesus, and the sayings of Paul and other writers of the New Testament contain the divine call to wisdom.

Need for Godly Wisdom

We know also from practical experience that we need our bodies and minds to have working relationships with the natural order around us, with other people, with social structures, and with foreseeable prospects. Therefore, to help us in this process of lifelong collaboration, we also need growth in wisdom. And to aid our growth in wisdom, we are given maxims for our guidance.

But, in view of our conflicting desires, our readiness to forget, and our gravitational pulls away from God and from what is best, much more than maxims are needed. We need that inner transformation of our desires by the supernatural action of the Holy Spirit which sets us on course toward the Kingdom of God and righteousness. In short, we must pray for what Wesley called "scriptural holiness," in addition to what we called earlier the supreme desire of the Christian, the love of God and neighbor.

But while this love aims us in the right direction, we require something else, namely, wisdom. Therefore, we are called by God to seek wisdom and to pray earnestly for the help we need in pursuing it. This divine summons is heard especially in God's call to love. The love of God and neighbor implies the quest for wisdom. If love is of God, so is wisdom. Therefore, wisdom, common sense, insight, sound judgment is an essential feature of Christian character.

Love motivates us to serve, but wisdom shows us how.

Knowing How to Love

Why does the love of God and neighbor imply wisdom? Because we do not know whether we are truly or effectively serving God and neighbor without godly wisdom. Christian love is purposeful. It has a job to do. Christ came seeking the well-being of those in need. So the question is: How can the purpose or aim of love be realized? Love can motivate us to serve, but wisdom shows us how.

If we say we love someone and yet keep on making foolish mistakes which adversely affect that person's life, what good is that love? Sometimes it is difficult to know which people do more harm, the bad or the mistaken. Just because a person "means well," or just because one has "pure intentions," does not indicate a responsible love. The right motive, which is love, may issue in harmful deeds if not executed through godly wisdom. We have heard the saying that the road to hell is paved with good intentions. The fact is that love implies wisdom and is apt to be merely sentimentality without it. A mother and father may "love" their children while doing (not responsibly assisting with) their elementary school assignments for them. But that kind of love incapacitates the children for solid achievements in reading, writing, and arithmetic. What could an enemy do that would be a greater obstacle to their children's future? People may "love" each other and be unwilling to seek wise counsel when they have demonstrated their inability to handle their deep and dangerous conflicts. What kind of love is that?

Whereas love is the answer to pride and selfishness, wisdom is the answer to folly.

The Partnership of Wisdom and Love

There are two basic problems in us which have to be faced to live a life guided by wisdom. One is the age-old problem of pride and selfishness. Except for a legitimate self-interest, self-centeredness and pride strike against the revealed purpose of God for our lives. Paul, Augustine, Luther, Calvin, Wesley, and many others have called attention to the biblical teaching on this "radical evil" in human nature. But not as much has been said about the second problem, namely, the tendency toward bad judgment and folly. Yet, this also strikes against the revealed purpose of God for us. If love, or right desire, is the answer to pride and selfishness, wisdom and common sense are the answers to our folly.

I am not suggesting here that we shall ever reach a stage of perfect wisdom in this life. Even when we love God and neighbor, we are liable to make mistakes. Indeed, even when we love ourselves, we make mistakes. This is partly because we do not know—and often cannot know—enough about the situations in which decisions have to be made. Sometimes we think we have made mistakes when in fact there were no

What we must promise God is to think-conforming our minds to God's-before we speak or act.

good options. Hence, whatever we may do will be followed by regrets. As we look toward the future, our vision is blurred. As we look back, our mistakes loom large to haunt us. But let us never forget that often we blame ourselves for decisions which might have been the best we could have done under the circumstances. Here the better part of wisdom is to forget our past mistakes—except to learn from them—and move into the future with earnest prayer for wisdom. In all of these practical matters, the "law of the best possible" obtains. God does not expect us to do more than the best we can. In the light of all this, we can see that God's call to wisdom requires both our daily and our lifelong response. And God promises help because God is the Lord of truth and wisdom. What we must promise God is to think—conforming our minds to God's—before we speak or act.

This calls for the habits of orienting our minds toward reality in practical matters. There is merit in the practice of consulting persons who know more than we do. This is what we do in relation to our physicians. And even when we do our best to seek the ways of practical good sense, there are times when we simply have to muddle through. In what areas are we called upon to manifest wisdom? In our family relationships, in the choice of schools, in the selection of a vocation, in our choice of a life-partner, in our work for a living, in our recreation, in all times of major decisions, and above all, in our selection of the church in which we want to experience and express our love of Christ.

It might be supposed that the attainment of practical good sense is an easy matter. All we need to do is make progress day by day. But it is not so simple. Just as we require the grace of God to enter upon the new life of love, so we must receive God's help in overcoming our strong tendencies toward prejudice, stupidity, and folly. Not enough attention has been paid to the obstacles to wisdom. For if we do not know the obstacles, how can we come to grips with them?

In the Bible we find many statements that show a keen awareness of the seriousness of the evils brought on by human foolishness. One writer speaking for wisdom says, "All who hate me love death" (Proverbs 8:36). We are told that those who love God "hate every false way" (Psalms 119:104, 128). Jesus spoke of "a wise man who built his house upon the rock" and of "a foolish man who built his house upon the sand" (Matthew 7:24-27). Accordingly, Jesus calls us to think and act wisely with our God-given gift of mind and reason. Therefore he included in the commandment to love God the words "with all your mind" (Matthew 22:37).

Obstacles to Wisdom

Let us consider now some of the main obstacles to wisdom or common sense and then reflect on how prayer can help us to overcome them. For one thing, our very pride and selfishness often lead us to foolishness. The ability to make sound judgments is often corrupted by wrongness within. This is why John Calvin said, "Our reason is overwhelmed with deceptions in so many forms, . . . stumbles at so many impediments, and is embarrassed in so many difficulties, that it is very far from being a certain guide" David Hume said: "Reason is the slave of the passions." And it has often been observed that the clue to our inconsistencies lies in our emotions. How many wars have been fought because pride overcame wisdom! How many homes have been broken and how many lives destroyed because self-love trampled upon essential sanity!

Again, and closely related to this, is the obstacle of the closed mind. Here a person will not listen to any view but his or her own. A person who will not learn is no better off than one who cannot learn. This too is tied to our beloved egos. Whenever our ideas are challenged, we try to defend them because they are ours rather than because they are true.

Another obstacle to wisdom and common sense is prejudice.

When we pray, we open ourselves in our relationship with God, to godly wisdom.

Prejudice is holding to ideas on the basis of our likes and dislikes rather than on the basis of the facts. Who can estimate the disasters to people's lives which were brought on because they failed to ask the simple question: What are the facts? What good is it to say, "I love the Lord and I love my fellow human beings," then in the next breath to say of the members of another race, "You are inferior"? The question is: What are the facts about all of those involved? It all comes down to orienting our minds toward reality and moving beyond what we prefer.

Still another obstacle to wisdom and common sense is what I call "the tyranny of the immediate present." What is immediately before us is so fascinating, bewitching, and compelling that we thrust from our minds any considerations for a longer view. We do this unconsciously or half-consciously, without realizing what we are doing. We are dazzled by the present, the now, by what is immediately before us. In other words, what is right before us might blind us to the larger and more far-reaching concerns. Personal, national, and world disasters have often resulted from this kind of breakdown of intelligence. Likewise, such a breakdown of intelligence threatens our own true security today.

One more obstacle to wisdom and common sense is wandering of mind. Wesley addressed the problems brought on by this in his sermon entitled, *Wandering Thoughts*. This is a universal problem in our human nature, and it has far-reaching effects on our practical judgment. We daydream our way through life. We are fascinated by our reveries, by sentimental hopes disconnected from concrete action, and the life of wisdom becomes impossible. In a kind of sleep-walking, half-conscious way, we keep our minds from thinking, reflecting, asking pertinent questions. Our minds are often not oriented toward reality because they are lost in our wandering thoughts.

In prayer, God helps us to overcome the obstacles to wisdom and to see things as God sees them.

Seeking Wisdom in Prayer

Where does prayer come into all this? Before responding to this question, I want to make one point clear. I am not here referring to academic or theoretical intelligence. College and university work is important, and so is the work of scholars. But learned scholars and teachers are in danger of the obstacles to wisdom as much as the unlearned. Nor am I speaking of a high IQ. When I speak of wisdom and common sense, I am referring to something everyone can attain in some degree. But it requires the willingness to stop and think, to ask such questions as these: What are the facts? Am I overlooking something important? Whose judgment might help me here? Should I wait a day, a week, or a longer period before deciding? What will happen, if I do this or that? Any normal person can stop and ask such questions.

Marshal Foch, the head of the Allied Forces in World War I, said something long ago which ought to be remembered by us today and for the rest of our lives. He said that all great battles have been lost because of the neglect of obvious matters. So is it in life. Wisdom is needed in all areas of our lives. It is needed in planning each day. It is required in managing our interpersonal relations, in, earning a living in saving and spending money, in what we choose to read and see and in the care of our bodies. Wisdom is needed especially in our understanding of the Bible, for it is our guide to life here and to heaven when we die. In all realms, we need the inspiration and guidance of the Holy Spirit. But we need to pray especially for the Spirit to reveal the things of God by giving us godly wisdom.

The enemies of wisdom and common sense are all around us and within us. But when we pray, we enter into a living relationship with the God of truth who hates needless ignorance and who despises prejudice. So when we pray, we feel ourselves to be in the presence of the One who understands us, our fellow human beings, and all things as they really are. Hence, we pray to God and ask for God's help in overcoming the obstacles to wisdom and to enable us to grow in the practice of orienting our minds toward reality.

Moreover, when we make mistakes of judgment and lapse into folly, in prayer we repent of our sin, ask God to forgive us, and decide to take another crack at using our God-given intelligence. In no case are we justified before God in saying, "Oh well, that was just an error of the mind, not of the heart." Both are sinful. In prayer, as we feel ourselves in the presence of the God of truth, we become keenly aware that breakdowns in intelligence and lapses in common sense are sinful. These too are morally wrong in the sight of God. So in prayer we repent before God for our foolishness and ask for God's help in using our minds more effectively. Only in this way can the work of love be done.

Prayer helps also by keeping us from being overly remorseful about our mistakes. No one is perfect. Everyone makes mistakes and will continue to do so. But, with God's help, we can reduce their number and their consequences. Through prayer we receive from the Lord of truth the encouragement and strength we need to improve ourselves in straight thinking. So we are reminded of the words of Scripture:

> *If you need wisdom, if you want to know what God wants you to do, ask him, and he will gladly tell you. He will not resent your asking.*
>
> **James 1:5 NLT**

In prayer we behold the glory of dedicating our minds not only to our own affairs but also to the affairs of Christ and his Church. For there too wisdom is required in order to carry forward God's work. Both in this realm and in the ongoing of our lives, one of our daily prayers should be:

> *Teach us to make the most of our time, so that we may grow in wisdom.*
>
> **Psalm 90:12 NLT**

Questions for Reflection

1. In what ways is godly wisdom different from the wisdom of the world? Who are people you know with godly wisdom and what makes this evident?

2. When have you lacked godly wisdom that led to your foolish acts?

3. When have you prayed for wisdom and discernment in making important decisions? How were your actions impacted?

person-to-Person Connection

One of the practices of the Levites was before making an important decision, they would pray for one week to seek God's wisdom and guidance on the matter.

Before making an important decision, prepare for the decision by seeking God's guidance and wisdom by praying daily for at least a week before acting.

Nineteen

Prayer and Science

There are many sciences: astronomy, geology, physics, chemistry, biology, biochemistry, microbiology, psychology, social sciences, et cetera. They are known as sciences because they share in the determination to practice methods of verification which are considered essential for arriving at truth. The sciences, though differing widely in fields of specialization, are similar in the steps required for verifying their theories. They begin with a problem to be investigated. They proceed by collecting data, suggesting hypotheses, performing relevant experiments, testing and retesting the hypotheses, and arriving at conclusions drawn from the total process. Sciences are communal studies.

It would not be going too far to say that the discovery of the scientific methods is one of the finest achievements of human beings. Science has freed us from numberless superstitions regarding diseases, natural disasters, future events, and environmental realities. It has made possible thousands upon thousands of conveniences and technologically based inventions, tools, and machines that save the time and energy of people around the world. Science and technology together have allowed us to envision realistically a world free from poverty, famine, and major diseases. The future of our world depends on the uses made of the many discoveries laid before the nations. But, are the advances in chemistry to be used for chemical warfare? Are the nuclear arsenals to be developed and used for destroying people and their cities?

Struggle Between Prayer and Science

What has all this to do with prayer? A great deal. According to many thinkers today–including some scientists and philosophers–prayer is considered superstitious. To be sure, there have been outstanding scientists in the past who believed in God and the life of prayer. So is it with many first-rate scientists and philosophers today. But there are many who believe that there is no scientific or rational basis for the practice of prayer, and for that reason they rule it out. In addition to many scholars who are either agnostics or philosophical naturalists, there are multitudes of others who, though not technically trained in the sciences, live in an atmosphere of doubt which leaves no place for prayer. They may say *yes* to meditation, but *no* to prayer. There are several reasons why people feel this way.

Those who breathe the atmosphere of doubt which pervades much of our culture seem to me to be what Wesley called "practical atheists." Even when they may believe in some kind of God, they act as if God did not exist. Another way of putting it is this: Many people are secularists, or ones who believe that if God is, God doesn't matter.

Many people–including some scientists–live in an atmosphere of doubt that leaves no room for prayer.

Consider now the many scientists and philosophers who have no place for prayer in their outlook and practice. One reason for thinking as they do is that they are so impressed with the

advances made by the sciences that they minimize or even
exclude other avenues of arriving at truth. Therefore, they
assume that any beliefs not derived from scientific method
and direct observation are to be laid aside.

Moreover, many scientists are apt to forget the limitations
that scientific method imposes upon itself. Among these
is the confinement to limited areas of investigation. The
scientific process, in proving or disproving theories, proceeds
by restricting radically its focus. Consequently, the scientific
process only deals with certain aspects or fragments of reality
at a time. Each science shuts out the total realms of reality
which lie around its special focus. In this way, the ultimate
questions are thrust aside as though they were irrelevant.
By their own principles, all sciences proceed by selecting
aspects of reality for exploration. However, theologians and
philosophers deal with reality as a whole: therefore they speak
of God as the Ultimate World Ground of it all.

The Ultimate Reality

Einstein said–what philosophers have known since Plato and
Aristotle: *The eternal mystery of the world is its comprehensibility.*
Amazingly, the physical world is intelligible to human minds.
This is only one important explantion of why scientists and all
persons need the benefit of theologians and philosophers.

Alfred North Whitehead made much of this. Science is made
possible because of the ordered processes with which it deals.
This is assumed in all types of experimentation and laboratory
work. But how do we explain an ordered universe when there
are infinite possibilities for chaos? There is no reason why

scientists and theologians might not join hands in believing in the Ultimate Mind who created and orders the universe and its varied and intricate processes. And whenever this happens, at least there is an open door to prayer for those who so believe.

Scientists and theologians as human beings should join hands in believing in the Ultimate Mind who created and orders the universe—which will open the door for prayer.

Closely related to these considerations is another factor of some importance. There are areas of reality and truth other than those with which the sciences deal. To be sure, scientists are fully aware of the extensive areas of potential knowledge not yet attained by the sciences. There are vast realms of unknowns. There are numberless gaps or chasms yet to be explored or which may never be explored. This fact has led some cynical scholars to say that religious people hold on to a "god of the gaps." As scientific knowledge advances, we keep receding into the realms of the unknown. Again, cynical scholars insist that here, in these gaps of human knowledge, is where God is still at work. So we Christians are charged with using God to fill in the vast chasms of human ignorance.

In response to this charge, two comments are in order. First, sound thought leads us to see clearly that these chasms of ignorance are a result of our lack of knowledge, not in the universe itself. Ultimately viewed, the God who created and sustains the universe acts in it and through it, in all of its known and unknown processes, to produce the whole ordered realm of reality. A "god of the gaps" is no god at all. This assumption leads to the point that if we do away with the gaps of ignorance, then there will be less and less point in talking about God. But, God cannot and should not be limited to the mere gaps in our human understanding regarding the ordering of things. For our best thinking leads us to see that any ordered universe requires the ultimate ordering of God–the Ultimate Mind or Intelligence–to explain its very existence and processes.

> *Where were you when I laid the earth's foundation? Tell me, if you understand. Who marked off its dimensions? Surely you know! Who stretched a measuring line across it? On what were its footings set, or who laid its cornerstone while the morning stars sang together and all the angels shouted for joy?*
>
> **Job 38: 4-7 NIV**

The second comment is that God is the Ultimate Reality and cannot be defined, and therefore limited, by science. God is not discoverable by any scientific method. God is a Spirit. Why should we assume that scientific methods alone lead human beings to orient themselves rightly to reality? There may be realms of reality that may never be discovered by the sciences. Music, poetry, novels, drama, morality, linguistics, history, and philosophical and theological reflections on the meaning of human life deal in reality also. And the saints have reported on what they have confirmed in the ongoing of their lives as the reality, presence, and power of God in prayer.

The Different Realm of Prayer

We are never justified in ruling out the realm of God's grace because we do not see how it can be made accessible to the sciences. When it comes to prayer, we move into a different realm from what can be scientifically verified. The realities of prayer cannot be stated in mathematical formulas. They cannot be put into test tubes or laid out on the tables of anatomy. Those who have experimented most persistently and resourcefully in the life of prayer speak most authoritatively on the subject. Everything here depends on the reality and love of God. If God is, and if God cares, then the doors to prayer are wide open. And all are invited to "taste and see that the Lord is good." There is then, no conflict between the faith that leads to the life of prayer and the whole realm of scientific truth. Both point to the Ultimate Reality which we know is the God of Truth and Grace.

Questions for Reflection

1. How do we sometimes limit God to those areas of life we do not understand?

2. When have you experienced God using scientific knowledge in others to bring about a Kingdom purpose (such as healing, etc.)?

3. When you have witnessed the power of prayer "breaking in" and even surprising the work of people rooted in the sciences?

person-to-Person Connection

God gives to humanity wisdom and understanding to make miraculous strides in the areas of science.

Pray for God's miraculous revelation to open understanding in an area in which you are passionate or deeply concerned– such as a medical or environmental breakthrough. Pray, by faith, that scientists (such as medical or environmental scientists) will be given supernatural knowledge and wisdom to bring forth the Kingdom of God.

Twenty

Unanswered Prayer

The great characters of the Bible were all familiar with the disconcerting experience of unanswered prayer. Moses prayed for God to let him go over the Jordan River into the Promised Land, but God did not grant his petition

> *At that time I pleaded with the LORD and said, "O Sovereign Lord, I am your servant. You have only begun to show me your greatness and power. Is there any god in heaven or on earth who can perform such great deeds as yours? Please let me cross the Jordan to see the wonderful land on the other side, the beautiful hill country and the Lebanon mountains." But the LORD was angry with me because of you, and he would not listen to me. "That's enough!" He ordered. "Speak of it no more. You can go to Pisgah Peak and view the land in every direction, but you may not cross the Jordan River."*
>
> **Deuteronomy 3:23-27 NLT**

This is exceedingly baffling to us when we consider all that Moses had done to deliver the people from slavery and to lead them creatively through the wilderness for forty years.

Job knew the anguish of unanswered prayer:

> *I cry to you and you do not answer me. I stand, and you merely look at me*
>
> **Job 30:20 NRSV**

And the psalmist searched aimlessly for God in times of trouble:

Why, O Lord, do you stand far off? Why do you hide yourself in times of trouble?

Psalm 10:1 NRSV

Even God told Isaiah that there would be times when it would seem to Isaiah that God was absent.

When you stretch out your hands, I will hide my eyes from you; even though you make many prayers, I will not listen; your hands are full of blood.

Isaiah 1:15 NRSV

In the New Testament, we also read of this same experience of unanswered prayer. Jesus himself prayed at Gethsemane saying, "My Father, if it be possible, let this cup pass from me." (Matthew 26:39). And Paul prayed three times for God to remove what he called a "thorn in the flesh." But that petition was denied him.

But to keep me from getting puffed up, I was given a thorn in my flesh, a messenger from Satan to torment me and keep me from getting proud. Three different times I begged the Lord to take it away.

Second Corinthians 12:7-8 NLT

If this happened to Moses, Job, the Psalmists, Isaiah, Jesus and Paul, it can happen to us.

Why Does It Go Unanswered?

Christians across the years and at all places and callings have shared in this experience of unanswered prayer. But, what are we to say about it? Are there any illuminating insights? The plain fact is that we cannot add much to what has been said already on this subject. Nevertheless, we may refresh our minds by looking at some of the ideas with which we are already familiar.

For one thing, everyone knows that there is such a thing as insincere prayer. Those who pray falsely do not really love God and neighbor. They do not truly want God's will to be done in them. Instead, because of some personal concern or danger from which they want to be delivered, they send out desperate prayers to God. In their desperation they may even make promises to God which they are not apt to keep. Only God can judge whether a prayer is sincere. Sometimes our prayers are mere words which we repeat ceremoniously. Jesus said,

> *When you pray, don't babble on and on as people of other religions do. They think their prayers are answered only by repeating their words again and again.*
>
> **Matthew 6:7** NLT

In the light of Christ, we know that this much is sure: No prayer is fully authentic that is not based on his command to pray for God's kingdom to come and for God's will to be done on earth as it is in heaven. The central reality in prayer is that not our will but God's will be done. This is at the heart of all true prayer.

At the heart of all true prayer is that God's will–not our will–be done.

Perhaps our prayers are not answered because we are unwilling to do our part. We pray God to forgive us for our sins, but we have not really decided to change our evil ways. Or, we have ignored the demands of Jesus, who said that if we are unwilling to forgive others who have wronged us, then God will not pardon our sins. We have to ask ourselves again and again whether we are actually praying in the name or spirit of the Master.

Or maybe when we pray, we ask God to do for us what God expects us to do for ourselves. There are many things which God never intended us to receive through prayer, for they must be the products of our own efforts. We should pray for daily bread, but that is no substitute for the skill of the farmers who cultivate the soil, plant the seeds, and bring in the harvest, nor should that prayer make us neglect the trips to the grocery stores.

Our prayers may not be answered yet because we are not ready for the answer!

I shall never forget the time when, as a ministerial student, I was praying earnestly for higher levels of Christian experience. As I did, the sure impression was given me by the Holy Spirit that I was expecting God to create Christian growth without my own creative efforts. God has given us minds to be used, hearts to be made alive, and wills to be set in motion. That was for me a real moment of illumination. Wesley was right when he said that a growing Christian is a Christian who keeps learning and reading. God never intended for prayer to be a substitute for the hard tasks of thinking and working. At the same time, these are no substitutes for the divine grace which comes to us through prayer.

And it may be that we do not receive what we ask for because we are not ready for it. God knows the stages of our spiritual development, and God may hold in reserve the divine responses until we have grown to adulthood. A little girl might ask for food which her mother knows she is not ready to digest. God, in infinite love and goodness, may give an answer to prayer by saying, "Not yet," or "not now."

How often it is that we pray for things and experiences which we would not know how to handle if we got them! A little boy might pray for a gun, but he ought not to have it. So it can be with the petitions of adults. Are we really ready for what we are praying for? That question is often overlooked.

Understanding Our Need

Frequently we do not know what to pray for because we do not know what we most need. In some moods we want one thing, in other moods we want the opposite. What would happen if God were to answer our every whim which comes to utterance in prayer! Our limited understanding–nay, our ignorance–is surely a factor in unanswered prayer. Oscar Wilde had a point when he said in *An Ideal Husband,* "When the gods wish to punish us, they answer our prayers." How often we are ruined by our own wishes!

Another thing to bear in mind is that God takes the laws of nature seriously. God established them and shows no signs of doing away with them. Fortunately for us, we can rely on the functioning of these steadfast ordinances. Of course, God's actions are not confined to the laws of nature, for God's grace moves dynamically beyond the realm of physical processes. But God does not defy the ordered systems. Therefore, some prayers are not answered simply because, if they were, the ordered universe would be disrupted. God wants us to live in full respect for the laws of nature which are essential to our health and well-being.

Beyond the Asking

The most important thing to remember about unanswered prayer is that it concerns only a small part of true prayer. Petition is only one part of prayer. In defining prayer we noted that it is essentially communion and encounter with God. We are to build our relationships with God through prayer. What if any other of our human relationships were strictly defined by our asking for what we want, or even what we need? But our relationship with God, through our prayers, is so much more!

Petition is only one part of true prayer.

If this is so, then almost all sincere prayers are answered. For those who truly seek God in the right way feel the divine presence. They walk with God, commune with God, and glory in God's presence. To be sure, there are times when God seems to hide from us. There is "the dark night of the soul" of which the saints have spoken. But, as people persist in prayer, the new day dawns, and God is again known and felt to be present in peace, joy, confrontation, and inner witness.

We may say, then, that when we do our part, there are some kinds of prayers which are always answered. One of these is the prayer for a life surrendered to and placed at the disposal of our heavenly Father. Another prayer which is invariably answered whenever we fulfill the conditions is the prayer for a life-long faith-relationship with God through Christ. Still another prayer which is always answered, when we do our part, is the prayer for forgiveness.

If we confess our sins, he who is faithful and just, will forgive our sins and cleanse us from all unrighteousness.
First John 1:9 NRSV

And the prayer for empowerment by the Holy Spirit so we can more effectively do the work of the Kingdom is always answered.

I believe the main reason for unanswered prayer is that we do not really pray for the things we most need. We have not, because we ask not. The most important prayer, and thus, the most important answer to prayer, is a closer walk with God and the desire to know and do God's will.

Questions for Reflection

1. How did you feel about your relationship with God when your prayers have gone unanswered?

2. When have you had an unanswered prayer that you later were thankful was not answered?

3. In what ways can you ensure your prayer life is more than petition? How can you re-focus your prayer life to be more about strengthening your relationship with God?

4. When was a seeming unanswered prayer really a "not yet" when it was answered later?

person-to-Person Connection

The psalmist reminds us:

> *Take delight in the Lord,*
> *and he will give you your heart's desire.*
>
> **Psalm 37:4 NLT**

God so desires to give us the desires of our heart, but we must first desire a relationship with God. In doing so, our hearts are more conformed to the heart of God and God's desires become our own.

Think of a petition you have placed before the Lord which has not yet been answered. Pray seeking God's desire on this matter. Read the Bible to understand better what God's heart desires. Then continue to pray, desiring most to cling to God, trusting God to answer your petition accordingly.

Twenty-one

Prayer and the Promise of Heaven

There are solid reasons for believing in personal immortality. The Old Testament pointed to it. The New Testament taught it. Jesus affirmed it. The apostles proclaimed it. And above all, God revealed the plan when he raised Jesus from the grave to conquer and redeem us. Therefore, against the background of that Easter morning, the following words of Jesus on the life everlasting have an abiding significance:

> *Because I live, you will live also.*
>
> John 14:19 NIV

> *I am the resurrection and the life. Those who believe in me, even though they die like everyone else, will live again.*
>
> John 11:25 NLT

These words become meaningful in our experience during times of worship and prayer.

Besides these biblical foundations for the belief in life after death, there is another one that should be mentioned. The loving, caring God we worship is not a being who, after creating us and placing us in a magnificent world, would simply give up his faithful children to cold nothingness. Moreover, God who created the universe and human beings for a purpose, who redeems people through Christ, who empowers them by the Holy Spirit, would not let all the value of these vast divine processes melt into nothing. It is absurdly illogical to think that a loving God would allow death to get the last word. God desires to be in relationship with us–even into eternity.

Death is no problem for God. Since God is wholly good and all-powerful, God will see to it that those who hold fast to God enter into the life everlasting. Philosophically speaking, the main reason for believing in the life after death is based on the goodness and power of God. But our final ground is the Bible. God has spoken, and what God has revealed in the Holy Word, God will bring to pass.

At a session of the American Philosophical Association, I met again Professor Charles Hartshorne, who for a number of years was a member of the department of philosophy at Emory University. He is generally considered to be the foremost exponent of process philosophy since Alfred North Whitehead. At the close of a lecture on immortality, to which he was a respondent, I asked Professor Hartshorne: Is there a process philosopher or theologian who believes in personal immortality? He replied: "I know of one who is trying to move in that direction." Then, after hesitating a moment, he added, "No. I cannot think of one."

Through Boston University I had the privilege of taking a course under Alfred North Whitehead. It was entitled "Cosmologies, Ancient and Modern." After class once, I said to him, "Professor, I know you believe in God, but why?"

He responded in one word, "Creativity."

"Creativity." What a word for the mind to explore! Turn anywhere, and there it is. I saw it in the Boston Garden where even a tiny yellow flower in perfection told of God. I saw God in the stars of Boston's cold nights, and I saw God as I thought of Mars and Jupiter and Saturn playing around the sun. And back down to earth, I saw God in the little sailboats on the Charles River.

"Creativity" in books with photographs of farmlands where seed and soil connived with sun and rain to put food on our tables.

"Creativity" where I saw God in books and libraries, colleges and universities, arts and sciences, and in Symphony Hall where human beings worked in near perfection in the production of beauty through music.

"Creativity!" I saw God in history where, at Bunker Hill men gave their lives for liberty. Finally, I saw God at Trinity Church where Phillips Brooks poured out his creative sermons on this grateful congregations.

All this does go far to satisfy the mind, but unfortunately not the soul. There must be the God who knows and feels that each human being is of supreme worth regardless of where we live, how old we are, our gender and the color of our skin.

Two types of theology and philosophy are at work here. On the one hand, Pantheism and Panentheism hold that each human personality is merged in God's Being or cosmic process. On the other hand, according to my theology, each finite person is given by God his or her own selfhood, self-identity and individuality which makes possible the person-to-Person connection we seek.

Therefore, the supposed contribution to God by Panthesists and Panentheists seems trivial to me in comparison with the marvelous interpersonal relationship we as God's children will have with God throughout eternity.

The practical question that arises now is this: How can our belief in the life everlasting become a dynamic force in our daily living? Often we feel the "reasons" of the heart where God speaks intimately, personally, and intuitively. We need to feel within us the presence of the Risen Lord. And yet these theological reasons still may not bring home to our hearts the experienced assurance of God's plan to conquer death and to lead us into everlasting adventures with God in heaven. So the question is: How can we, in our everyday lives, experience and anticipate the power and the glory of the life after death?

Our God, who is true to us in prayer, will not be untrue to us in death.

The answer is that this comes through prayer. For as we walk with God, we enter into an experienced relationship which we feel and know cannot be broken by death. For God will not allow it. In the life-giving relationship with our God, we receive the mysterious, wonderful assurance that God has claimed us both for this life and the next. Our heavenly Father, who is true to us in prayer, will not be untrue to us in death. In prayer, then, the belief in heaven becomes a living hope that shapes and colors our entire existence.

Through prayer we also gain intimations of what heaven will be like. Many people want to think of heaven as a place, a setting, an environment. The biblical images of the pearly gates, the streets of gold, the jasper walls, and the crystal sea are taken literally as described in Revelation 21:18 and 21. To be sure, there is a true meaning here. What the inspired writer is saying, it seems to me, is that heaven is a new dimension of existence, unutterably beautiful and magnificent.

More than a Place

We cannot think of any life after death which does not have some kind of environment. Biblical writers speak of this as "a new heaven and a new earth" (Revelation 21:1 and also Second Peter 3:13). Jesus referred to the setting in these words:

> *There are many rooms in my Father's home, and I am going to prepare a place for you. If this were not so, I would tell you plainly.*
>
> *When everything is ready, I will come and get you, so that you will always be with me where I am.*
>
> John 14:2-3 NIV

The main point is that God will provide a new environment–called heaven–where his children can grow, adventure, and rejoice with God and with those who love God.

In prayer we learn that the environment is not the main thing. Heaven must be some kind of magnificent place where there will be the "many rooms." But most important, heaven is more than a place: Heaven is a mysterious, dynamic relationship with God that begins here and is nurtured now by faith. Heaven is also an opportunity for creative work and sharing.

In prayer these deeper meanings of our life together with God in heaven move from the merely theoretical and abstract into the experienced now.

In prayer we come to understand that heaven is a new relationship of love for God. It is joy in the presence of God. It is hope for opportunities with God. It is adoration of God. It is glorying in God's presence. It is peace unspeakable. It is the never-ending summons to growth and creative advance. All these and numberless other features of heaven are hinted at in prayer. And in prayer the sublime words of Jesus move deep into our hearts:

> *Do not let your hearts be troubled. Believe in God, believe also in me.*
>
> **John 14:1 NRSV**

Through the inspiration of the Holy Spirit, the biblical vision of heaven and our prayer life come together in a mysterious harmony that provides a deep abiding peace.

Glorious Future Fuels the Present

There is another important connection between prayer and the hope of heaven. Through prayer, the anticipation of the life with God after death becomes a primary dynamic for service in the here and now. For some people the hope of a glorious future in heaven lures them away from the responsibilities of today. But this cannot happen in true prayer. For when we Christians pray, we do so with Jesus Christ before us. We pray in his name, with a true concern for the physical and spiritual needs of people now. As we anticipate heaven to pray and to have fellowship with the God and Father of our Lord Jesus Christ is to identify ourselves with the needs of people whom Christ lived and died to save. Indeed, any authentic hope of heaven is made manifest by our love of God and of our fellow human beings. Our deeds do not function as the power of God's great salvation through faith in Jesus Christ Crucified and Risen. But they are among the surest signs of being saved.

The great question is: Are we being prepared for Eternity?

Plato sided with the Psalmist (103:15) in reminding us of the shortness of our life on earth. That ancient Greek put it this way:

The whole period of three score years and ten is surely but a little thing in comparison with eternity.

And cynics who contemplate these realities might say that we are stranded between the cold and barren peaks of two eternities. Nevertheless, in God's Word we are promised that in our brief time on earth, in one holy moment of faith in Jesus Christ we can receive God's gift of the life everlasting. Our time on earth is for preparation for our tomorrows. Supremely, the meaning of our time on earth is preparation for eternity with God and with those who love God in heaven.

Paul brought all of this together magnificently when, after referring to the glories of the life to come, he reminded the Corinthians of their present duties. He said:

Therefore, my beloved brethren, be steadfast, immovable, always abounding in the work of the Lord, knowing that in the Lord your labor is not in vain.
First Corinthians 15:58 NLT

I like the words, "abounding in the work of the Lord." When, through prayer, we experience the vital hope of heaven, there is present in us the new dynamic for service to others. By grace we long to follow Jesus in being people for others, both in this life and in the life to come.

So in prayer we glory in the future. For Jesus Christ, our Risen Lord, has opened the door for us to enter the portals of heaven and join the community of all the saints. We celebrate, in anticipation, the heaven that was prepared for us from the foundation of the world. At the same time, we glory in the present. For we now experience with God, through Jesus Christ, the intimations of the heaven yet to come.

Questions for Reflection

1. When you envision heaven, what is it that you hope for?

2. How do your prayers reflect this foundational hope for an everlasting relationship with God and all the saints?

3. How could your prayers propel you to prepare for heaven in the here and now?

person-to-Person Connection

Life–both here and now and in eternity–is ultimately all about our relationship with God and one another.

Ask God to help you reshape your prayer life to prepare you to bring about God's Kingdom here on earth through you in your preparation for heaven. Then begin to see daily how, enriched by your prayers, you can bring about God's Kingdom one small act, one relationship, one day at a time.

References of Quoted Material

Chapter One

Henry Francis Lyte (June 1, 1793–November 20, 1847) was an Anglican theologian and hymn-writer. He wrote this hymn only three weeks before his death from tuberculosis.

Abide With Me; fast falls the eventide;
The darkness deepens; Lord with me abide.
When other helpers fail and comforts flee,
Help of the helpless, O abide with me.

Swift to its close ebbs out life's little day;
Earth's joys grow dim; its glories pass away;
Change and decay in all around I see;
O Thou who changest not, abide with me.

Not a brief glance I beg, a passing word;
But as Thou dwell'st with Thy disciples, Lord,
Familiar, condescending, patient, free.
Come not to sojourn, but abide with me.

Come not in terrors, as the King of kings,
But kind and good, with healing in Thy wings,
Tears for all woes, a heart for every plea—
Come, Friend of sinners, and thus bide with me.

Thou on my head in early youth didst smile;
And, though rebellious and perverse meanwhile,
Thou hast not left me, oft as I left Thee,
On to the close, O Lord, abide with me.

I need Thy presence every passing hour.
What but Thy grace can foil the tempter's power?

Who, like Thyself, my guide and stay can be?
Through cloud and sunshine, Lord, abide with me.

I fear no foe, with Thee at hand to bless;
Ills have no weight, and tears no bitterness.
Where is death's sting? Where, grave, thy victory?
I triumph still, if Thou abide with me.

Hold Thou Thy cross before my closing eyes;
Shine through the gloom and point me to the skies.
Heaven's morning breaks, and earth's vain shadows flee;
In life, in death, O Lord, abide with me.

Immanuel Kant (April 22, 1724–February 12, 1804) was a German philosopher from Königsberg in East Prussia (now Kaliningrad, Russia).

John Wesley (June 28, 1703–March 2, 1791) was an eighteenth-century Anglican minister and Christian theologian and founder of the renewal movement that became the Methodist church. "Inward holiness" leading to "outward holiness" is one of the basic principles of Wesleyan theology.

The quote on page 31 is from Wesley's sermon titled: *Upon Our Lord's Sermon on the Mount.* It is Sermon No. 8 based upon the text from Matthew 6:19-23. Here is the quoted material in context of the sermon.

Indeed experience is here so full, strong, and undeniable, that it makes all other arguments needless. Appeal we therefore to fact. Are the rich and great the only happy men? And is each of them more or less happy in proportion to his measure of riches? Are they happy at all? I had well nigh said, they are of all men most miserable! Rich man, for once, speak the truth from thy heart. Speak, both for thyself, and for thy brethren!
Amidst our plenty something still,–
To me, to thee, to him is wanting!
That cruel something unpossessed

Corrodes and leavens all the rest.
Yea, and so it will, till thy wearisome days of vanity are shut up in the night of death.

Surely then, to trust in riches for happiness is the greatest folly of all that are under the sun! Are you not convinced of this? Is it possible you should still expect to find happiness in money or all it can procure? What! Can silver and gold, and eating and drinking, and horses and servants, and glittering apparel, and diversions and pleasures (as they are called) make thee happy? They can as soon make thee immortal!

William James (January 11, 1842–August 26, 1910) was a U.S. psychologist and philosopher. He published his *Principles of Psychology* in 1890. This quote is from *Principles of Psychology*, I, page 316.

Chapter Two

Friedrich Heiler (1892–1967) was a German theologian and historian of religion. This quote is from *Prayer* (New York: Oxford University Press, 1958), pages 119-121.

Chapter Three

Borden Parker Bowne (1847-1910) was an American Christian philosopher. The quote is from page 27 of his book, *Personalism*, published in 1908.

Augustine (November 13, 354–August 28, 430) was one of the most important figures in the development of Western Christianity. This quote is from his *Confessions*, IX, iv.

Martin Luther (November 10, 1483–February 18, 1546) was a German monk, theologian, and church reformer. Quote from *Luther's Works*, volume 10, page 45.

Chapter Four

Jeremiah has been called "the first man of prayer known to the history of religion" and "the father of true prayer," from Heiler, *Prayer*, page 122.

Chapter Five

Heiler quote about Paul from *Prayer*, page 124.

Chapter Six

William Hazlitt (April 10, 1778–September 18, 1830) was an English writer. This quote is from *The Complete Works of William Hazlitt*, published in London by JM Dent and Sons, Ltd., Vol. 6, page 184.

Chapter Seven

Socrates (around 470 BC–399 BC) was an ancient Greek philosopher who is widely credited for laying the foundation for Western philosophy. His best known quote is "Know Thyself."

John Donne (1572–1631) Preached December 12, 1626. *Eighty Sermons*, no. 80, sct. 3, published in 1640.

Wesley's Sermon 41, *Wandering Thoughts*.

Chapter Eight

William Shakespeare (baptised April 26, 1564–April 23, 1616) *Hamlet* was published in 1603. This quote is from Act I, Scene 4.

Wesley's Sermon 13, *Sin in Believers*.

Chapter Ten

Matthew Arnold, this poem was first published in 1857.

To Marguerite: Continued
Yes! in the sea of life enisled,

With echoing straits between us thrown,
Dotting the shoreless watery wild,
We mortal millions live alone.
The islands feel the enclasping flow,
And then their endless bounds they know.

But when the moon their hollows lights,
And they are swept by balms of spring,
And in their glens, on starry nights,
The nightingales divinely sing;
And lovely notes, from shore to shore,
Across the sounds and channels pour--

Oh! then a longing like despair
Is to their farthest caverns sent;
For surely once, they feel, we were
Parts of a single continent!
Now round us spreads the watery plain--
Oh might our marges meet again!

Who order'd, that their longing's fire
Should be, as soon as kindled, cool'd?
Who renters vain their deep desire?--
A God, a God their severance ruled!
And bade betwixt their shores to be
The unplumb'd, salt, estranging sea.

Alfred North Whitehead (February 15, 1861–December 30, 1947) English mathematician and philosopher. Quote from a lecture given at Harvard University on March 13, 1926.

Chapter Eleven

John Milton (December 9, 1608–November 8, 1674) was an English poet. The reference is to *Paradise Lost,* his epic poem published in 1667.

Sigmund Freud (May 6, 1856–September 23, 1939), was an Austrian neurologist and psychiatrist. His works were published widely in the late nineteenth and twentieth centuries.

Chapter Fourteen

Wesley experienced the anew power of God's saving grave during a Bible study on Aldersgate Street in London on May 24, 1738. He wrote in his journal:

> **In the evening I went very unwillingly to a society in Aldersgate Street, where one was reading Luther's preface to the Epistle to the Romans. About a quarter before nine, while the leader was describing the change which God works in the heart through faith in Christ, I felt my heart strangely warmed. I felt I did trust in Christ alone for salvation; and an assurance was given me that He had taken away my sins, even mine, and saved me from the law of sin and death.**

Chapter Fifteen

Martin Luther Quote from *Luther's Works*, volume 10, page 45.

Chapter Sixteen

Leo Tolstoy (September 9 1828–November 20 1910), was a Russian writer.

Joseph Fort Newton (July 21, 1876–January 24, 1950) was a well-known preacher, pastor and author.

Chapter Seventeen

Augustine from *City of God* III, 21.
Second quotation also from *City of God, XIX, 19*

Alfred North Whitehead, *Adventures of Ideas,* 1933.

Chapter Eighteen

John Calvin (July 10, 1509–May 27, 1564) was a French Protestant theologian during the Protestant Reformation and was a central developer of the system of Christian theology called Calvinism or Reformed theology. This comment is from *Institutes of the Christian Religion*, II, 2, xxv. It was first published in 1536.

David Hume (April 26, 1711–August 25, 1776) was a Scottish philosopher, economist, and historian.

Wesley's Sermon 41, *Wandering Thoughts*.

Marshal Ferdinand Foch (October 2, 1851–March 20, 1929) a French soldier, was the supreme commander of allied forces during World War I.

Chapter Nineteen

Albert Einstein (March 14, 1879–April 18, 1955) was a German-born theoretical physicist. Quote is from "Physics and Reality" in *Franklin Journal*, 221: (1936), page 351.

Chapter Twenty

Oscar Wilde (October 16, 1854–November 30, 1900) was an Irish playwright, novelist, poet, and author of short stories. The play was published in 1895.

Chapter Twenty-one

Charles Hartshorne (June 5, 1897–October 9, 2000) was a prominent American philosopher of religion and developer of process theology. Personal encounter with the author.

Plato (428 or 427 BC–348 or 347 BC), was an ancient Greek philosopher, who along with Socrates and Aristotle laid the philosophical foundations of Western culture. He said this statement in Book X of his *Republic*.

PLOWPOINT
Breaking Ground for the Seed of the Gospel

Other Resources Available

- *Checking Vital Signs: assessing your local church potential*
  A guide to lead your church through finding the potential God has given you for ministry in your community.
- *Feeding and Leading of Shepherds: learning to relate as sheep and shepherds.*
  Designed to reclaim and strengthen the biblical call and ministry of spiritual leaders as shepherds of the flock.
- *Longing to Belong: learning to relate as the body of Christ*
  A ten week study designed to equip the church and church leaders to respond to conflict while strengthening our relationships with Jesus Christ and one another.
- *person-to-Person: building a relationship with God through prayer*
  An easy-to-read, yet comprehensive study of prayer, what prayer is and how to grow in your prayer-life.
- *Stepping in the Stream: learning to relate to the will of God.* A guide for individual, congregational, and ministry team discernment of God's vision with practical "next steps" to put the vision into action.

Easy Ways to Order

Fill out the form below and send it in by any of the means listed here:
PO Box 979 Graham NC 27253
Phone 336.226.0282 Fax 336.226.5894
Toll-free 866.269.2421
resources@plowpoint.org
www.plowpoint.org

Name:
Address:
City, State, ZIP
Phone Number:
Email:
Please send me the following: